Grades 4-8

NotebookReference

Writer's Guide Second Edition

● ●

School Specialty® Publishing

Send all inquiries to:
School Specialty Publishing
8720 Orion Place
Columbus, OH 43240-2111

ISBN 0-7696-4345-0

1 2 3 4 5 6 7 8 9 10 PAT 10 09 08 07 06

TABLE OF CONTENTS

SECTION I
GRAMMAR

In the following section you will find a grammar guide explaining each of the eight parts of speech. Keep reading to learn how to identify and use the parts of speech correctly. Knowing grammar will help you to improve every part of your writing.

THE EIGHT PARTS OF SPEECH

Parts of speech are categories of words. The categories are based on how words are used in a sentence. Many words can fit into more than one category. For example, *round* can be an adjective, noun, verb, adverb, or preposition.

A marble is *round*.
We sang a *round*.
Round these numbers to the nearest tenth.
Gather *round*.
The worried parents waited *round* the telephone.

In English, there are eight parts of speech.

1. **NOUNS** name a person, place, thing, or idea.
child, James, school, tree, courage

2. **PRONOUNS** take the place of nouns.
they, me, hers, herself, who, those

3. **VERBS** show action or a state of being.
tackle, think, am, was

4. **ADJECTIVES** describe a noun or pronoun.
shiny, happier, best

5. **ADVERBS** modify a verb, an adjective, or another adverb.
well, carefully, very

6. **PREPOSITIONS** show the position or relationship between a noun and another word.
over, from, in spite of

7. **CONJUNCTIONS** connect words or phrases.
and, yet, but, or, neither/nor

8. **INTERJECTIONS** show emotion.
Ouch! Yikes! Hooray!

NOUNS

A **noun** names a person, a place, a thing, or an idea. There are several different types of nouns.

Singular and Plural Nouns

A **singular noun** names one person, place, or thing.

> boy, park, swing

A **plural noun** names more than one person, place, or thing.

> cups, plates, bowls

Plural Noun Rules

- To change most singular nouns to plural nouns, add *s*.
  > cups, bowls
- To nouns ending in *s*, *ch*, *sh*, or *x*, add *es*.
  > buses, peaches, dishes, taxes
- To nouns ending in *y* after a vowel, add *s*.
  > days, keys
- To nouns ending in *y* after a consonant, change the *y* to *i* and add *es*.
  > parties, flies
- To nouns ending in *o* after a vowel, add *s*.
  > rodeos, radios
- To nouns ending in *o* after a consonant, add *es*.
  > potatoes, tomatoes
- Words that refer to music are exceptions.
  > pianos, solos
- To some nouns ending in *f* or *fe*, change the *f* or *fe* to *ves*. You need to memorize or look up which nouns to change.
  > safes, knives, roofs, leaves
- Some nouns, including many animals, have irregular plurals.
  > children, feet, mice, deer

Common and Proper Nouns

A **common noun** is a word that names any person, place, or thing. Common nouns do not begin with a capital letter unless they are the first word of a sentence.

> river, country, boy, girl, dog, school

A **proper noun** is a word that names a special person, place, or thing. Proper nouns begin with a capital letter.

> Ohio River, Mexico, Danny, Amy, Spot, Center Middle School

Abstract and Concrete Nouns

An **abstract noun** names an idea, quality, or state of mind.

> peace, patience, success, sadness

A **concrete noun** names something that can be seen or touched.

> road, flower, house, animal, Joe

Possessive Nouns

A **possessive noun** shows ownership. It tells who or what owns something. To make a singular noun show possession or ownership, add an apostrophe and an *s*.

Jason—Jason's ball
Carla—Carla's dress
Maggie—Maggie's book

To make a plural noun show possession or ownership, add an apostrophe after the final *s*.

girls—girls' basketballs
parks—parks' benches

If the plural noun does not end in *s*, add an apostrophe and an *s* as you would for a singular noun.

children—children's
men—men's

Collective Nouns

A **collective noun** names a group of people, places, or things. When a collective noun refers to a group as a unit, it is considered singular. When it refers to the individual members of the group that are acting separately, it is considered plural.

singular collective nouns:
The *school* of fish lives in the cool water.
Our *team* usually wins.

plural collective nouns:
The *school* of fish are all swimming in different directions.
The *team* are all expected to earn good grades.

Some common collective nouns are: *assortment, gang, collection, crowd, group, herd, crew, band, batch, pile, set, troop, bunch, team, pride of lions, gaggle of geese, school of fish, murder of crows, swarm of bees, pack of dogs, flock of sheep.*

Predicate Nouns

A **predicate noun** is a noun that comes after a linking verb and refers back to the subject. It is used as a subject complement. (The subject of the sentence and the predicate noun represent the same thing.)

Leo was the fiercest *lion* in the zoo.

Noun Clauses

A **noun clause** is a dependent clause that functions as a noun. It may be used as a subject, a direct object, an indirect object, an object of a preposition, or a predicate noun.

subject: *What occurred* was not planned at all.
direct object: They wondered *what they should do* now.
indirect object: Should they make *whoever broke the window* pay the bill?
object of the preposition: They were grateful to *whomever cleaned up the mess.*
predicate noun: The good thing was *that no one was hurt.*

Appositives

An **appositive** is a noun or noun phrase placed next to or very near another noun or noun phrase. It identifies, explains, or adds to its meaning or renames the initial noun or pronoun.

Bones, *the scaffolding of the body*, are tied together with ligaments.

PRONOUNS

A **pronoun** takes the place of a noun. Every pronoun has an **antecedent**. An antecedent is the noun that a pronoun refers to or replaces. A pronoun must agree with its antecedent in number, person, and gender.

>*Juan* shined his shoes after *he* walked through the mud.
>The *girls* are baking the cake *they* promised to make for the fundraiser.

When a singular pronoun is followed by another pronoun, the second pronoun must also be singular. The following are all singular pronouns:

someone	anyone	everyone	none	each
somebody	anybody	everybody	nobody	everything

>**Incorrect:** Everybody has finished *their* assignment.
>**Correct:** Everybody has finished *his* or *her* assignment.
>**Incorrect:** Has anyone finished *their* dinner?
>**Correct:** Has anyone finished *his* or *her* dinner?

Personal Pronouns
Personal pronouns name the speaker, the person spoken to, or the person or thing spoken about. They are:

singular: I, my, mine, he, his, him, she, her, hers, it, its you, your, yours

plural: we, our, ours, us you, your, yours they, them, their, theirs

Relative Pronouns
The pronouns *that, which,* and *who* are called **relative pronouns**.
Use *who* when speaking of people.

>The girl *who* arrived is my sister.

Use *which* when including extra information about animals or things that is not needed to understand the sentence. Set off these *which* phrases with commas.

>His dog, *which* is a Dalmatian, has won many awards.

Use *that* when speaking of people, things, or animals.

>The house *that* we live in is painted blue.

Subject Pronouns
Use a **subject pronoun** (*I, you, he, she, it, we, they*) when the pronoun is the subject of a sentence or clause.

>*He* said Aunt Ellen would come at 2:00.
>*They* were worried when *she* didn't come.

Pronouns that follow the verb *be* restate the subject, so they need to be subject pronouns.

>"Who is *it*?" asked the Third Little Pig.
>"It is *I*!" snarled the Big Bad Wolf.
>"It is *he*!" gasped the other two pigs.

Object Pronouns
Use an **object pronoun** (me, you, him, her, it, us, them) when the pronoun directly

receives the action of a verb.

> Aunt Ellen called *them* later.

Use an object pronoun when the pronoun indirectly receives the action of a verb.

> Aunt Ellen sent *us* flowers.

Use an object pronoun when the pronoun is the object of a preposition.

> Uncle Charlie took a picture of *her*.

Intensive Pronouns

An **intensive pronoun** emphasizes, or intensifies, the noun or pronoun it refers to. An intensive pronoun can be omitted. It is optional.

> The children *themselves* designed this playground.
> The owner *himself* took us on the tour.

Reflexive Pronouns

A **reflexive pronoun** refers the action back to the noun or pronoun. A reflexive pronoun is not optional. Omitting it changes the meaning or makes the sentence incomplete.

> She reminded *herself* not to mention the surprise party.

Possessive Pronouns

A **possessive pronoun** is one that shows ownership or possession. Possessive pronouns include *my, mine, your, yours, his, her, its, our, ours, their, theirs.*

> He forgot *his* homework as he raced out of school.

Indefinite Pronouns

An **indefinite pronoun** is one that refers generally, not specifically, to people, places, or things. Some indefinite pronouns are always singular, some are always plural, and some may be either singular or plural.

> singular indefinite pronouns: *anyone, everyone, no one, someone, something*
> plural indefinite pronouns: *many, both, few, several, others*
> singular or plural indefinite pronouns: *all, any, most, some, none*

Predicate Pronouns

A **subject complement** is a word that comes after a linking verb and refers back to the subject. When a pronoun is used, it is called a **predicate pronoun**.

> That flashlight is *hers*.

Interrogative Pronouns

An **interrogative pronoun** introduces a question. *Who, what, which, when, how,* and *why* are common interrogative pronouns.

> *What* event does Becky plan to enter?
> *Which* school will Manuel choose?

Demonstrative Pronouns

A **demonstrative pronoun** shows, or demonstrates, which noun is being talked about in the sentence. *That, these, this,* and *those* are demonstrative pronouns. Be careful! Because these four words can also be adjectives, a demonstrative pronoun has to take the place of a specific noun.

> demonstrative pronoun: Please load *this* and *that* onto the truck.
> adjective: *Those* shoes are too dirty for you to come in *this* house.

VERBS

All **verbs** help make a statement. Most verbs help make a statement by showing action.

> Jack *cooked* dinner.

Verbs can also show a state of being.

> She *looks* worried.

Action Verbs

An **action verb** shows action. It shows what someone or something does, did, or will do.

> Grandmother and I *baked* a cake.
> Cheryl *plays* softball every afternoon.

Linking Verbs

Other verbs help show the appearance or condition of something. These verbs are called **linking verbs**. Linking verbs connect, or link, the subject of the sentence to a word or words in the predicate.

> Her dress *is* lovely.

The verb *to be* is the most common linking verb.

> present: I am, we are   past: I was, we were
> you are   you were
> he is, she is, it is, they are   he was, she was, it was, they were

Any verb that can be substituted by a form of *to be* is a linking verb. Other common linking verbs are: *seem, become, appear, remain, look,* and *feel*.

Helping Verbs

Sometimes a sentence needs more than one verb to make the statement clear. These words are called **helping verbs**.

> common helping verbs: *am, are, is, was, were, do, did, have, has, had, can, may*

A **verb phrase** contains one or more helping verbs along with the main verb.

> Terry *had drawn* a beautiful picture.
> William *must have worn* an overcoat.
> *Were* the children *walking* to school?

Transitive and Intransitive Verbs

A **transitive verb** is an action verb that is followed by a direct object. The verb "transmits" the action from the subject to the object.

An **intransitive verb** does not need an object to complete its meaning. It is often followed by a prepositional phrase.

> transitive: We *caught* a fish.
> intransitive: I *fish* with my dad.

Infinitives

An **infinitive** is a present tense verb that follows the word *to* (to + verb = infinitive). An infinitive can act as a noun, an adjective, or an adverb.

> George sat on the front step *to finish* his ice-cream cone.

An **infinitive phrase** includes modifiers, a complement, or a subject, which act together

as a single part of speech.

> subject: *To make dinner* for Grandma was Lesley's reason for taking a cooking class.
> predicate noun: Lesley's hope is *to make a seven-course meal.*

Gerunds

A **gerund** is a verb form ending in *ing* that functions as a noun. Adding *ing* to a verb in the present tense forms a gerund. A **gerund phrase** is a group of words that includes a gerund and its related words.

> gerund: *Dancing* is my favorite form of exercise.
> gerund phrase: *Dancing the polka* is a good workout.

Participles

A **participle** is a verb form that can function as an adjective. Adding *ing* to a present tense verb usually forms the present participle. The past participle is usually formed by adding *ed* to the present tense. A **participial phrase** is a group of words that includes the participle and its objects, complements, or modifiers.

> present participle: Rex barks at the *passing* cars.
> past participle: A *determined* Rex tried to chase the car.

Verb Tense

Verb tense shows the time in which the action takes place. There are six tenses: present, past, future, present perfect, past perfect, and future perfect.

Present tense shows action or a state of being that is happening now.

> I *eat* chocolate.

Past tense shows an action or state of being that has been completed.

> I *ate* chocolate.

Future tense shows action or a state of being that will take place. The helping verb *will* is usually used with the principal verb to form the future tense.

> I *will eat* chocolate.

The **present-perfect tense** is formed using the present tense of the helping verb *to have* plus the past tense of the verb it helps. This combination is called the **past participle**. Together, the tense they form is called the present-perfect tense.

> has (present tense of helping verb) + past participle action verb = present-perfect tense
> Our cousins *have arrived* at last.

The past tense of an action verb shows a definite time something happened in the past. The present-perfect tense shows an indefinite time when something happened and shows that it may still be going on.

> The cruise ship *arrived* late. (definite: *Late* answers when it arrived.)
> The cruise ship *has arrived.* (indefinite: *It* has arrived at some time.)

Because the two tenses are used to show a definite or indefinite action, you should be careful when mixing the two tenses.

> **Correct**: My dad told me to clean my room yesterday.
> > (*Yesterday* is a definite time.)
> **Incorrect:** My dad *has told* me to clean my room yesterday.
> > (*Has told* cannot be used to show a definite time, and *yesterday* is definite.)

The **past-perfect tense** is formed using the past tense of the verb *to have* plus the past participle.

> had (past tense of helping verb) + past participle action verb = past-perfect tense

When talking about things that have happened in the past, use the past-perfect tense to show which action happened first.

> Mike *went* to the restaurant.
> His friends *talked* about the restaurant.

Did the friends tell Mike that the restaurant was good before or after he went to the restaurant? Using the past-perfect tense shows which action happened first.

> His friends *talked* about the restaurant.
> Mike *had gone* to the restaurant.

The **future-perfect tense** is formed using the verbs *will* and *have* plus the past participle.

> will (auxiliary verb) + have (helping verb) + past participle = future perfect tense

Use the future-perfect tense to show the "future past." When talking about things that will happen in the future, the future-perfect tense shows that an action will be completed before another.

> My science project *is* due on Monday during fourth period.
> I *will have finished* the project by then.

In this example, the future-perfect tense shows that the project will be finished before it is due. The events will happen in the future, but one will happen first. This is the "future past."

Active and Passive Voice
A verb is in the **active voice** when the subject is performing the action.

> Mike *ate* the last piece of cake.

A verb is in the **passive voice** when the subject receives the action or is the result of the action.

> The last piece of cake *was eaten* by Mike.

Tip: Change sentences in passive voice to active voice whenever possible. Active voice is much stronger than passive voice, and using active voice will make your writing clearer and more exciting.

Subject–Verb Agreement Rules
One of the most important parts of writing sentences is making a subject and its verb agree. Most of us can tell the difference between which verb to use (*like* or *likes*) in a simple sentence such as this: Jose *likes* to draw. Sentences with compound subjects, tricky pronouns, or collective nouns are more difficult. Here are some guidelines to help you.

- Singular subjects use singular verbs. Plural subjects use plural verbs.
  > Jen *likes* chicken.
  > All the kids *like* chicken.
- Compound subjects connected by *and* use a plural verb.
  > Mike and Karen *play* soccer.
- Compound subjects connected by *or* use a singular verb if the subject following *or* is singular and a plural verb if the subject following *or* is plural.
  > Who knows where or when it *will rain*.
  > How or why they *changed* the show I don't know.

- Most indefinite pronouns are singular and require a singular verb.
  *anyone, anything, each, either, everybody, everyone, everything,
  neither, no one, nothing, one, someone, something*
- Some indefinite pronouns can be singular or plural depending on the use.
  both, few, many, others, several
- Most collective nouns require a singular verb because the group acts as one.
  audience, bunch, class, family, group, herd, pack, set, team
- If a group is divided and its members are acting as individuals, it may use a plural noun.

Irregular Verbs

Irregular verbs form their tenses by a change in spelling or word form. The only way to know irregular verbs is to use and memorize them. Most verbs follow the regular rules. There are only about 50 irregular verbs. Some of them are:

be	do	go	run	teach
become	draw	grow	say	tear
begin	drink	know	see	think
blow	drive	lay (put down)	set	throw
break	eat	lead (guide)	shake	wear
burn	fight	lend	sing	write
burst	fly	lie (recline)	speak	
choose	forget	lie (tell a lie)	steal	
come	freeze	lose	strike	
dive	get	rise	swim	

ADJECTIVES

An **adjective** is a word that describes a noun or pronoun in three ways.
An adjective tells **what kind**.

> The *fluffy* yellow duckling looked for its mother.

An adjective tells **which one**.

> *That* boy is in my class this year.

An adjective tells **how many**.

> I'll give you *several* reasons why you must write two reports.

Positive, Comparative, and Superlative Adjectives

Some adjectives are used to compare nouns. The **positive adjective** describes a noun or pronoun without comparing it to anyone or anything else. A **comparative adjective** is used to describe a comparison between two things, people, places, or actions. A **superlative adjective** compares three or more things, people, places, or actions.

	positive	comparative	superlative
adjectives	happy	happier	happiest
	good	better	best

Demonstrative Adjectives

This, *that*, *these*, and *those* are **demonstrative adjectives** that modify nouns by telling "which one" or "which ones." *This* and *that* are singular. *These* and *those* are plural. *This* and *these* refer to things nearby, and *that* and *those* refer to things farther away.

> *This* zoo we are visiting is the best in the state.
> *That* zoo across town isn't nearly as nice.
> *These* animals we are seeing are cared for very well.
> *Those* animals over there are not cared for as well.

Indefinite Adjectives

An **indefinite adjective** is an adjective that gives an estimated number or quantity or that refers to no specific person or thing. It does not tell exactly how many or how much.

> When we go out, we bring a *few* snacks to share with each other.

Articles

A, *an*, and *the* are special adjectives called **articles**. They are used to describe a singular noun. The word *a* is used before a word that begins with a consonant sound, and the word *an* is used before a word that begins with a vowel sound.

> *A* bunny is nesting under *the* porch.
> *The* baby bunnies are eating up *the* garden.

Predicate Adjectives

A **subject complement** is a word that comes after a linking verb and refers back to the subject. An adjective used as a subject complement is called a predicate adjective. A **predicate adjective** follows a linking verb and describes the subject.

> Laura's flashlight is *bright*.

ADVERBS

An **adverb** is a word that usually describes a verb. It can also describe an adjective or another adverb.

An adverb tells **how**.
> The boy ran *fast*.

An adverb tells **when**.
> Dinner will be ready at *five o'clock*.

An adverb tells **where**.
> Joshua played *nearby*.

An adverb tells **how often**.
> Julie takes dance lessons *daily*.

Positive, Comparative, and Superlative Adverbs

Adverbs, like adjectives, have three degrees of comparison. The **positive adverb** describes a noun, pronoun, or adjective without comparing it to anyone or anything else. A **comparative adverb** is used to describe a comparison between two things, people, places, or actions. A **superlative adverb** compares three or more things, people, places, or actions. Some adverbs form the comparative degree by adding *er* and the superlative degree by adding *est*. Most adverbs that end in *ly* form their comparative degrees by adding the words *more* or *less* in front of the positive degree. Adding the words *most* or *least* in front of the positive degree forms the superlative.

> Raquel danced *less gracefully* than her sisters.
> I hope they will come *sooner* rather than *later*.

	positive	comparatives	superlatives
adverbs	happily	more/less happily	most/least happily
	well	better	best
	fast	faster	fastest

Adverb Clauses

An **adverb clause** is a dependent clause that functions as an adverb. It can modify verbs, adjectives, or other adverbs and tells *where, when, in what manner, to what extent, under what condition,* or *why*.

> We dress warmly *when we play in the snow*.

Qualifying Adverbs

Adverbs can modify other adverbs. These adverbs are called **qualifying adverbs**. They strengthen or weaken the adverbs they modify. They answer the questions *how much* or *to what extent*.

> He walked on the ice *very carefully*.
> (*Very* strengthens the adverb *carefully*.)
> No one on the field trip knew *quite exactly* where to find the bus.
> (*Quite* weakens the adverb *exactly*.)

PREPOSITIONS

A **preposition** is a connecting word. It connects ideas. A preposition also shows the relationship between a noun or pronoun and some other word or idea in the sentence.

A preposition shows **time**.
> *before, after, during, until, while, since*

A preposition shows **direction**.
> *across, toward, from, around, behind*

A preposition shows **cause**.
> *on account of, in spite of, due to, because of, since*

A preposition shows **position**.
> *above, against, beneath, on, over, under, inside*

Prepositional Phrases

A **prepositional phrase** is a group of words starting with a preposition. The phrase usually ends with a noun or pronoun. It can function as an adjective or an adverb, depending on the word it modifies. Like a one-word adjective, an adjective prepositional phrase modifies only a noun or a pronoun.

> I heard the news *on the radio*.
> Rita reached *into the bag*.

A sentence may have more than one prepositional phrase.

> I listened *to the news* *on* the radio.
> Rita reached *into* the bag *for* an apple.

Like a one-word adverb, an adverb prepositional phrase usually modifies a verb and may tell where, how, or when an action takes place.

> The White House is located *in Washington, DC*. (tells where)
> The president resides there *with his family members*. (tells how)
> He will leave the White House *at the end of his term*. (tells when)

Object of the Proposition

The noun or pronoun used as the **object of the preposition** follows the preposition or prepositional phrase. A preposition relates the noun or pronoun to another word in the sentence.

Introductory Phrases

Many **introductory phrases** and clauses begin with a preposition. Use a comma to separate these phrases from the rest of the sentence.

> *Because* I am sick, I will not be able to go on the field trip.

List of Prepositions

aboard	considering	from between	in regard to	outside
alongside	despite	from under	inside	over to
away from	down from	in addition to	instead of	regarding
behind	except for	in front of	on account of	underneath
besides	from among	in place of	on behalf of	within

CONJUNCTIONS

Conjunctions are connecting words. They can connect words, phrases, or sentences. *And, or, but, for,* and *yet* are all conjunctions. Use conjunctions to combine subjects, predicates, or two smaller, related sentences. This helps your writing to flow more smoothly.

Compound subject:

Cindy is learning to surf. I am learning to surf.

Cindy *and* I are learning to surf.

Compound predicate:

Cindy likes to surf. Cindy likes to skateboard.

Cindy likes to surf *and* skateboard.

Compound sentences:

Cindy likes to surf. She is getting better at it.

Cindy likes to surf, *and* she is getting better at it.

Coordinating and Subordinating Conjunctions

Conjunctions are words that join words or groups of words. *And, but, or, nor,* and *for* are **coordinating conjunctions** because they coordinate, or organize, the connection between two independent clauses.

Becky lives down the street, *and* we're going to her house after school.

Subordinating conjunctions show the connection between a dependent, or subordinating clause, and the rest of the sentence. *As, when, because, since, unless,* and *before* can be subordinating conjunctions. When the subordinating clause comes at the beginning of the sentence, a comma follows it.

I will iron. You are tired.

I will iron *whenever* you are tired.

Because you are tired, I will iron.

INTERJECTIONS

An **interjection** is a word that shows strong feeling.

Ouch! That really hurt!

Sometimes an interjection is a short phrase.

You're kidding! I would never go in that cave by myself.

An interjection begins with a capital letter, ends in an exclamation point, and is separate from a sentence.

Yikes!

Some words that are used as interjections are also used in sentences to show mild feeling. These are called **mild interjections**. When used this way, they are followed by a comma, not an exclamation point.

Oh, whoops, I dropped my books.

List of Interjections

Ouch!	Great!	Yes!	Please!	Not on your life!
Oh!	Well!	No!	Watch out!	Alright!
Aha!	Oh no!	Hurrah!	Of course!	Awesome!

SECTION 2
USAGE

Usage is how we use language correctly and properly. Although many neighborhoods and groups have their own patterns of informal speech, it is important that all students learn to speak and write standard English. Standard English is the language of educated people. Many people judge others by the way they speak. What would your initial reaction be to someone who said, "He don't know nothing"? This section on usage will help you write clear sentences, give you tips on using words correctly, and give you help with confusing pronouns.

WRITING SENTENCES WITH CLARITY

The Four Kinds of Sentences
There are four kinds of sentences.
A **declarative** sentence makes a statement. It should end in a period.
> Karen plays basketball.

An **imperative** sentence gives a command. It should end in a period.
> Karen, come here.

An **interrogative** sentence asks a question. It should end in a question mark.
> Where is Karen?

An **exclamatory** sentence shows surprise or strong emotion. It should end in an exclamation point.
> Karen's team won!

Clauses
An **independent clause** is a group of words with a subject and a predicate that states a complete thought and can stand by itself as a sentence. A **dependent clause** cannot stand alone. It depends on the independent clause of the sentence to complete its meaning. Dependent clauses start with words like *who, which, that, because, when, if, until, before,* and *after.*
> *When* we went to the school carnival, we saw lots of clowns.
>   (dependent)   (independent)

Fragments and Run-ons
Groups of words that do not tell or ask us something are called sentence **fragments**.
> fragment: the blue cup
> complete sentence: Randy drank cocoa from the blue cup.

Run-on sentences usually occur when end punctuation is left out of sentences. Always remember to put end punctuation at the end of a sentence.
> run-on: It was Donna's turn to bat she hit a home run what a sight!
> complete sentences: It was Donna's turn to bat. She hit a home run. What a sight!

Subjects and Predicates

Every sentence has two parts: the subject and the predicate. The **complete subject** consists of all the words in the sentence that describe what or who is being talked about. The **complete predicate** consists of all the words in the sentence that describe what the subject is doing, did, or will do.

My friend, Glenda, baby-sits every Saturday.
complete subject: My friend, Glenda
complete predicate: baby-sits every Saturday.

Simple Subjects and Predicates

The **simple subject** is the main word in the complete subject. The **simple predicate** or predicate verb is the main verb or verb phrase in the complete predicate.

My friend, Glenda, baby-sits every Saturday.
simple subject: Glenda
simple predicate: baby-sits

Compound Subjects and Predicates

A **compound subject** is made of two or more subjects that have the same verb and are joined by a conjunction such as *and* or *or*.

The king of Spain believed in the cities of gold.
The queen of Spain believed in the cities of gold.
compound subject: The king and queen of Spain believed in the cities of gold.

A **compound predicate** is two or more predicates that have the same subject and are joined by a conjunction.

The Spanish believed in a fairy tale.
The Spanish followed the legend of the cities of gold.
compound predicate: The Spanish believed a fairy tale and followed the legend of the cities of gold.

Both a compound subject and compound predicate can be in one sentence.

My sister *and* I   love to make *and* eat caramel apples.
(compound subject)   (compound predicate)

Simple, Compound, Complex, and Compound-Complex Sentences

A **simple sentence** contains one independent clause.

Maxwell is a sumo wrestler.

A **compound sentence** contains two independent clauses that are closely related. A comma and a conjunction or a semicolon usually connects the two clauses.

Clocks tell time. They are also used for decoration.
compound sentence: Clocks tell time, *but* they are also used for decoration.

A **complex sentence** contains an independent clause and one or more dependent clauses. A dependent clause often begins with a relative pronoun, such as *who, which, whose, that,* or *whom.*

The butterfly, <u>*whose wings were brightly colored*</u>, flitted from flower to flower.
(dependent clause)

A **compound-complex sentence** contains two or more independent clauses and at least one dependent clause.

> <u>*When* I get home from school</u>, I like to eat a sandwich, and I like to listen to music. (dependent clause)

Modifiers

The complete subject or complete predicate of a sentence usually contains words or phrases called **modifiers** that add to the meaning of the sentence.

> The ancient tombs, *which stand powerfully on the hot sands of Egypt*, are an amazing and wonderful sight.

Modifiers that are not placed near the words or phrases that they modify are called **misplaced modifiers**.

> **Misplaced:** *Scared to death*, the black night enveloped the lost student.
>
> **Correct:** *Scared to death*, the lost student wandered the neighborhood.

If a modifying word, phrase, or clause does not modify a particular word, then it is called a **dangling modifier**. Every modifier must have a word that it clearly modifies.

> **Dangling modifier:** *Warmed by the sun*, it felt good to be at the beach.
>   ("Warmed by the sun" does not modify "it.")
>
> **Correct:** *Warmed by the sun*, we relaxed on our beach towels.
>   ("Warmed by the sun" modifies "we.")

GUIDE TO MISUSED WORDS

a — an
The word *a* is used before a word that begins with a consonant sound.
> Danny painted *a* picture of his friends.

The word *an* is used before a word that begins with a vowel sound.
> Patty put *an* apple in her lunch sack.
> There is still *an* hour before lunch.

accept — except
The word *accept* is a verb that means to receive or to agree to.
> I *accept* your apology,

The word *except* is a preposition that means other than.
> You can take everything *except* the bike.

affect — effect
The word *affect* is a verb that means to influence.
> His inspirational words *affected* her deeply.

The word *effect* is a noun that refers to something brought on by a cause.
> What *effect* will the rain have on the baseball game?

already — all ready
Use the time word *already* to say that you have completed a task earlier.
> I *already* finished my homework.

Use the two words *all ready* to say that you are completely prepared.
> I am *all ready* to start my homework.

and — to
And is a conjunction that means also.
> Billy *and* I are going to the park.

To is used before a present-tense verb to form an infinitive. Don't use *and* instead of *to* in an infinitive.
> **Incorrect:** Come *and* get us at the park at 6:00.
> > Try *and* get a video we'll all like.
> **Correct:** Come *to* get us at the park at 6:00.
> > Try *to* get a video we'll all like.

between — among
Use the word *between* when speaking of two persons or things.
> Ryan must choose *between* a new soccer ball and a new baseball mitt.

Use the word *among* when speaking of more than two persons or things.
> The five groups split the history projects *among* themselves.

bring — take
The word *bring* means carry to.
> *Bring* the paper in from the porch.

The word *take* means carry away from.
> *Take* this report with you when you leave.

farther — further

The word *farther* is an adjective or adverb that means at a greater measurable distance or length. Think of the word *far*, which describes a long distance or length.

Jim can jump *farther* than Kevin can.

The word *further* is an adjective or adverb that means more distant in time or degree; additional.

How much *further* do we have to drive?

fewer — less

The word *fewer* refers to things that can be counted.

We had *fewer* plants than we thought.

The word *less* refers to things that can be measured.

The success of the show was *less* than expected.

good — well

Use the adjective *good* when describing a person or thing.

That was a *good* movie.

Use the adverb *well* when telling how something is done.

Dennis plays the trumpet *well*.

healthful — healthy

Healthful is used to describe things that promote good health.

Taking vitamins and eating *healthful* food is important.

Healthy is used to describe the state of being in good health.

I eat a balanced diet to remain *healthy*.

I — me

Use *I* in a compound subject when the speaker is part of the subject. A good test is to replace the compound with just *I*.

Correct: *Mike and I* played video games with Tony.

(Test: *I* played video games with Tony.)

Incorrect: *Mike and me* played video games with Tony.

(Test: *Me* played video games with Tony.)

Use *me* when the speaker receives the action of the verb. Again, a good test is to replace the compound with just *me*.

Correct: Mike loaned *Tony and me* his video game.

(Test: Mike loaned *me* his video game.)

in — into

Use *in* to refer to something inside a location.

The towels are on the top shelf *in* the linen closet.

Use *into* to refer to a movement from outside to inside a location.

Let's go *into* the restaurant—it's freezing out here!

Dave went *into* his bedroom to get a change of socks.

its — it's

Its is a possessive pronoun.

The dog sat next to *its* bone.

It's is a contraction of "it is."

> *It's* the perfect day for a picnic.

let — leave

Use the word *let* when speaking about allowing or permitting something.

> Will you *let* me ride your bike?

Use the word *leave* when speaking about going away from or to somewhere.

> We will *leave* for our meeting in one hour.

Also use *leave* to mean to allow to remain.

> **Correct:** *Leave* the tools by the peach tree.
> **Incorrect:** *Let* the boys alone!

lie — lay

The word *lie* is a verb that means "to rest or recline." The forms of *lie* are *lie, lies,* (is) *lying, lay,* and (have, has, or had) *lain.*

> Mark *will lie* on the sofa.
> Mark *is lying* on the sofa.
> He *lay* there for two hours.
> He *has lain* there for two hours.

The word *lay* is a verb that means "to put or place something." The forms of *lay* are *lay, lays, laying, laid,* and (have, has, or had) *laid.*

> Kathy, *lay* your coat on the bed.
> Kathy *is laying* her coat on the bed.
> She *laid* her coat on the bed.
> Kathy *has laid* her coat on the bed.

like — as if

Like is only a preposition. *Like* should never be followed by a verb.

> That sweater is just *like* one you already have.

Use *as if* as a subordinate conjunction to introduce a clause.

> It looks *as if* Gary and Nancy are getting along great.

loose — lose

Use the adjective *loose* to describe something that isn't tight.

> My tooth is *loose.*

Use the verb *lose* to mean not winning.

> We can't *lose* this game.

may — can

The word *may* is used when asking or giving permission.

> "*May* I borrow your math book?" asked Lisa.
> "Yes, you *may,*" said Sandra.

The word *can* is used when talking about being able to do something.

> "*Can* you jump rope?" asked Ben.
> "I *can* jump rope," said Jeannie.

of — off

The word *of* is used to mean belonging to something, containing something, or about something.

May I have a cup *of* milk?

Do not use the word *of* instead of *have*. Use *have* with the words *ought, must, might,* and *could*.

    Incorrect: He *could* of told me.

    Correct: He *could* have told me.

The word *off* is used to mean "away from" or "not on or touching" something.

    The dress fell *off* its hanger.

Do not use the word *off* instead of *from*.

    Incorrect: Helen borrowed some sugar *off* her neighbor.

    Correct: Helen borrowed some sugar *from* her neighbor.

Do not use the word *off* with the word *of*.

    Incorrect: Get *off of* the grass.

    Correct: Get *off* the grass.

principal — principle

A *principal* is the leader of a school. The princi*pal* is your *pal*.

    Our *principal*, Dr. Taylor, used to teach science.

When something is *principle*, it is important or first.

    The *principle* conductor never led the orchestra's rehearsals.

raise — rise

The word *raise* is a verb that means to "grow something" or "move upward." The forms of *raise* are *raise*(s), (is) *raising, raised,* and have *raised*.

    Ellen *is raising* the bottom shelf.

    We *will raise* tomatoes this year.

The word *rise* is a verb that means to "go up" or "get up." The forms of *rise* are *rise*(s), (is) *rising, rose,* and (have) *risen*.

    I *rise* at 6 each morning.

    The sun *has risen*.

say — go

Always use the word *say* instead of the informal *go* when writing dialogue or describing what someone said.

    Bad: "And then he *goes*, 'Whatever,' and just walks off."

    Better: "And then he *said*, 'Whatever' and just walked off."

since — because

The word *since* expresses a period of time.

    We've been swimming *since* 8 this morning.

The word *because* expresses a cause or reason.

    Correct: We're swimming *because* we love the exercise.

    Incorrect: We're swimming *since* we love it.

sit — set

The word *sit*(s) is used when speaking of resting or staying in one place.

    "Please, *sit* in the blue chair," said Mother.

    "Robby usually *sits* in the yellow chair," said Tony.

The word *set*(s) is used when speaking of putting or placing an object somewhere.
> Connie *set* the cups on the counter.
> She usually *sets* them in the sink.

that — which
Use *that* to introduce a clause without a comma.
> She took the bat *that* was signed by Cal Ripken.
Use *which* to introduce a clause following a comma.
> She stared at the bat, *which* lay broken on the floor, and burst into tears.

then — than
The word *then* means "at that time."
> We had dinner, and *then* we washed the dishes.
The word *than* introduces the second item in a comparison.
> I like the blue van better *than* the red sports car.

there — their — they're
The word *there* is used to mean in that place, to that place, or at that place.
> The ball rolled over *there*.
The word *there* is sometimes used with the words *is, are, was,* and *were.*
> *There* are five cookies on the plate.
The word *their* is used to show ownership or possession.
> The students picked up *their* books.
The word *they're* is a contraction. It means "they are."
> *They're* coming over tomorrow.

very — so
Both *very* and *so* can be used as adverbs, but do not use *so* in place of *very* to show amount or degree.
> **Incorrect:** Yuki is *so* cute.
> **Correct:** Yuki is *very* cute.

whose — who's
The word *whose* is a possessive pronoun.
> *Whose* is this cup?
The word *who's* is a contraction of "who is."
> *Who's* the owner of this cup?

your — you're
The word *your* is a possessive pronoun.
The word *you're* is a contraction of "you are."
> *You're* going to *your* lesson whether you like it or not!
> (you are)   (pronoun)

PRONOUN PROBLEMS

Polite Pronouns

One should be polite and always name oneself last. Therefore, "me and ___" is never correct. If the speaker is part of the subject, he or she should say "___ and I," as in "Jacob and I are allergic to cats." If the speaker receives the action of the verb or follows a preposition, he or she should say "___ and me," as in "Please give Chelsea and me any leftover candy."

Avoiding Sexist Pronouns

Pronouns must agree in number, person, and gender with the noun they refer to. Until recently, indefinite pronouns, such as *each* and *everyone*, used a masculine singular pronoun.

Everyone has a right to his own opinion.

However, many people today believe that there are different ways of changing language to make it more neutral and that not everyone agrees on the best way of doing so. Whenever possible, replace *he*, *him*, or *his* with *he or she*, *him or her*, or *his or hers*. Just remember that subject, verb, and pronoun must agree: don't use the plural "they" in a sentence with a singular subject.

Correct: Everyone has the right to *his or her* own opinion.
Incorrect: Everyone has the right to *their* own opinion.

Unnecessary Words

It may be tempting to add extra words, especially unnecessary pronouns, to sentences. To avoid making mistakes, reread each sentence and link the pronouns to their antecedents. If one antecedent has more than one pronoun, one may need to be removed. Here are some examples.

Incorrect: I saw that man there fixing a tire.
The word *there* is unnecessary because *that* already points out *the man*.
Correct: I saw that man fixing a tire.

Incorrect: Sam doesn't have himself a new pair of shoes for school.
Himself is unnecessary because it already says that *Sam* doesn't have the shoes.
Correct: Sam doesn't have a new pair of shoes for school.

Incorrect: These here pants are torn.
Here is unnecessary because *these* tells you which *pants*.
Correct: These pants are torn.

Incorrect: That girl at the movies she wouldn't sit down
The word *she* is unnecessary because *that* tells you which *girl*.
Correct: That girl at the movies wouldn't sit down.

Who vs. Whom

Although *whom* is being used less frequently in informal speech, its correct usage is still preferred in formal writing. Because *whom* sounds a little like *him*, it is easy to remember

that the difference between *who* and *whom* is the same as the difference between *he* and *him*. *Who* and *he* are subject pronouns. *Whom* and *him* are object pronouns.

> *Who* is your best friend? *He* is my best friend.
> *Whom* did you invite to your party? I invited *him*.

Direct and Indirect Objects

A **direct object** is a noun or pronoun that answers the question, "what?" or "whom?" after the verb.

> Andy watched the *parade*.
> What did Andy watch? He watched the parade.
> *Parade* is the direct object in this sentence.

> Jeff took *Kelly* to the library.
> Jeff took whom to the library? He took Kelly to the library.
> *Kelly* is the direct object in this sentence.

An **indirect object** is a word that tells "to whom" or "for whom" something is done. An indirect object usually comes between the verb and the direct object.

> Mother made *Sarah* a new dress.
> First, what did mother make? She made a new dress. *Dress* is the direct object.
> For whom did Mother make a new dress? She made it for Sarah.
> *Sarah* is the indirect object in this sentence.

SECTION 3
MECHANICS

Mechanics are the rules for capitalization and punctuation. All the rules you need to know to write a perfectly punctuated paper are right here. In this section, you'll find rules for using commas, periods, quotation marks, and many other punctuation marks, as well as rules for using italics and underlines. You'll also find suggestions for formatting your paper. "Formatting" explains how to punctuate paragraphs, how to make a title page, and where to put your name, the date, the page numbers, and other important information on a paper.

CAPITALIZATION

Rules for Capitalization
Use a capital letter at the beginning of a sentence.
> **W**e went to the space center today.

The first word in a greeting and the first word in a closing should be capitalized.
> **D**ear Mr. Jackson,
> **S**incerely, Tamara

A proper noun names a particular person, place, or thing. Every proper noun begins with a capital letter.
> **J**acob
> **C**enter **M**iddle **S**chool
> **J**upiter
> **T**een **M**agazine

The names of relatives, such as Father and Mother, should be capitalized when they are used as a name or with another name.
> Is **M**other home yet?
> Did **U**ncle **J**im call?

The first letter of titles and abbreviations of titles, such as Doctor and Mrs., should be capitalized.
> **D**octor Sanchez
> **M**r. Sanchez

Use a capital letter for initials that stand for someone's name.
> **J.F.** Kennedy
> **F.D.** Roosevelt

Every city name begins with a capital letter.
> **J**acksonville
> **S**an **D**iego

Every state name begins with a capital letter.
> **F**lorida
> **M**ichigan

The days of the week and the months of the year each start with a capital letter.
> **F**riday
> **J**anuary

The names of holidays begin with capital letters.
> **P**resident's **D**ay
> **M**emorial **D**ay

The first word, last word, and each important word in a book title begin with capital letters. Do not capitalize words like *a, an, and, at, by, for, in, of,* and *the* unless they are the first word of the title.
> **H**uckleberry **F**inn
> **T**rumpet of the **S**wans

The word *I* is always capitalized.
> Dave and **I** are going to the movies this afternoon.

When referring to the planet, *Earth* is capitalized. When referring to dirt, it is not capitalized.
> I enjoy studying about our planet, **E**arth, and its moon.
> The earth was dry and hard, so we used shovels and hoes to loosen the soil.

PUNCTUATION

Comma (,)

Use a comma after introductory words or phrases.

> Chris, I found your missing necklace.
> If we hurry, we can get to the bus stop in time.

Use a comma in a compound sentence—two complete thoughts joined by *and, but, or, yet,* or *for.*

> The rain poured outside the tent, but we were snug and dry in our sleeping bags.

Use a comma to separate three or more words in a series.

> Gold, silver, and copper are used to make jewelry.

Use a comma to separate three or more phrases in a series.

> Did you vacation at the beach, in the mountains, or on the ranch?

Use a comma to tell the reader to pause, or to separate the name of the person being spoken to from what is being said.

> Brandon, are you coming with us?
> Yes, my mom said I could go.

Use a comma in a date between the day of the month and the year, and after the year if the sentence continues.

> My birthday is October 30, 1992.
> On February 9, 1992, my little sister was born.

Use a comma between the city and the state, and after the state if the sentence continues.

> Kelly lives in Lexington, Kentucky.
> Kelly has lived in Lexington, Kentucky, for two years.

Use a comma after the greeting and the closing in a friendly letter.

> Dear Uncle Bob,
> I hope you are feeling much better.
> Sincerely,
> Naomi

Use a comma after the closing in a business letter.

> Yours truly,
> Samuel Foster

Semicolon (;)

Use a semicolon to combine two independent clauses in a compound sentence when a conjunction (*and, but, yet*) isn't used.

> Frank plays tennis; his sister is a swimmer.

Colon (:)

Use a colon to introduce a list or a series of things.

> For the hike, you will need the following items: sturdy shoes, thick socks, a water bottle, and a backpack.

Do not use a colon if the series follows an expression, such as *for example, namely, for instance,* or *that is.*

> We were pestered by flying insects, namely mosquitoes and black flies.

Use a colon to separate hours and minutes when writing the time.

> It is now 10:45 A.M.

Use a colon after the salutation or greeting in a business letter.

> Dear Mrs. Jennings:

Period (.)

Use a period at the end of a statement.

> I love to write.

Use a period at the end a command.

> Put the fried chicken in the picnic basket.

Use a period at the end a request.

> Please bring me that map.

Use a period after abbreviations, such as Mrs., Ave., and yd.

> Mrs. Roberts lives on Sabrina Ave.

Use a period after an initial.

> U.S. Grant was a Civil War general before he became president.

Exclamation Point (!)

Use an exclamation point at the end of a sentence that shows surprise or warning.

> Wow! You really surprised me just then.
> Watch out for falling rocks!

Question Mark (?)

Use a question mark at the end of an interrogative sentence.

> Are you going to the football game tonight?

Quotation Marks (" ")

Use quotations marks when writing exact words from a conversation. When the speaker's name comes first, use a comma before the quotations.

> Brent said, "That sounds really cool."

When the speaker's name comes last, use a comma, question mark, or exclamation point at the end of the quotation.

> "This is a special CD collection," answered Tony.
> "Why are you wearing a sling?" asked Alyshia.
> "Don't feed the bears!" warned Aaron.

When the speaker's name comes in the middle, use a comma before and after the name to separate it from the quotation.

> "Have you noticed," asked Julie, "that this playground is a mess?"

Put quotation marks around the titles of songs, poems, and stories.

> "Yellow Submarine" by the Beatles
> "Where the Sidewalk Ends" by Shel Silverstein
> "The Emperor's New Clothes" by Hans Christian Andersen

Parentheses ( )
Use parentheses to separate a list from the rest of a sentence.

> Bring your supplies (sack lunch, pencil, clipboard, worksheets) for the field trip.

Use parentheses to separate a phrase or clause from the rest of a sentence.

> Mark (who is Danny's big brother) walked into the store.

Brackets ( )
Use brackets in a quotation to replace a word or to explain a word.

> As Alice was falling and falling down the rabbit hole, she feared that she would never stop: "I must be getting somewhere near the centre (British spelling of *center*) of the Earth," she said to herself.

Use brackets to explain something that is already in parentheses.

> *Alice's Adventures in Wonderland* has been a favorite children's story ever since its publication over a century ago (it was first published in 1865 (Macmillan), but because of printing errors, it was reprinted a year later by a second New York publisher (Appleton)).

Apostrophe (')
Use an apostrophe in a contraction to take the place of one or more letters that are taken away.

> can't, won't, shouldn't

Use an apostrophe in a possessive noun to show what belongs to whom.

> Sheila's shoes, the children's coats, the brothers' skateboards

Hyphen (-)
Use a hyphen to break a word between syllables at the end of a line in running text. The dictionary will show you where it is appropriate to break a word.

> This is our fav-
> orite place to eat.

Use a hyphen to join two-part numbers.

> twenty-one, ninety-nine

Use a hyphen to separate a prefix from a proper noun.

> pro-American

Use a hyphen to write a fraction as a word.

> one-half

Use a hyphen to join some compound nouns and adjectives.
  hurricane-like weather, our favorite baby-sitter

Dash (—)

Use a dash to separate a list from the rest of a sentence.
  Bring your supplies—sack lunch, pencil, clipboard, and worksheets—for the field trip.

Use a dash to separate a phrase, clause, or list from the rest of the sentence.
  Mark—who is Danny's big brother—walked into the store.

Ellipsis Points (...)

Use ellipsis points to mark words you left out of a direct quote.
  "The rainforest is the greatest...source of carbon dioxide on Earth."

Slashes (/)

Use slashes to mark the line breaks in a poem or play dialogue you are quoting.
  "'Tis but thy name that is my enemy;/Thou art thyself" according to Shakespeare's
  Juliet.

ITALICS AND UNDERLINES

Italics (*italics***)**
Use italics on **book titles**.
    Huckleberry Finn

Use italics on **magazines**.
    Time

Use italics on **newspapers**.
    New York Times

Use italics on **pamphlets**.
    Facts About Skincare

Use italics on **play titles**.
    Romeo and Juliet

Use italics on **film titles**.
    101 Dalmatians

Use italics on **television programs**.
    Sesame Street

Use italics on **works of visual art**.
    da Vinci's *Mona Lisa*

Use italics on **comic strips**.
    Peanuts

Use italics on **software**.
    WordPerfect

Use italics on **names of ships**, **trains**, **aircraft**, **spacecraft**.
    Titanic, Silver Streak, Spirit of St. Louis, Columbia

Use italics for **words as words**.
    We painted a large sign that said *OPEN*.

Underline (Underline)
Book titles are always underlined when hand written. When they are typed, they should be italicized.
    I just read <u>Holes</u> by Louis Sachar.
    I just read *Holes* by Louis Sachar.

FORMATTING PARAGRAPHS AND PAPERS

Your teacher will probably give you guidelines on how to format your paper, but here are some ideas and reminders to help you prepare a professional paper:

- Prepare a **title page** with the title, your name, and the date. Do not underline or italicize your title unless your teacher tells you to do so.
- If you don't use a title page, write the **title** at the center of the top of the first page with your name underneath it. Write the **date** in the top right-hand corner of the paper.
- Start the **first paragraph** one line below your name.
- Start **each paragraph** with an **indented sentence**.
- Your teacher should tell you if you need to **single-space** or **double-space** your paper. Keep in mind that this will affect your **page count**.
- Write the **page number** either at the bottom center of each page or in the top right hand corner. Do not write the page number on the first page. Instead, write 2 on the second page and continue from there.
- If your paper has **visual aids** or **illustrations**, clearly divide them from the text or keep them on a separate page.
- At the end of your paper, include a separate page for your **bibliography**.
- Keep all the pages of your paper together in a **folder** or use a **paper clip** or a **binder clip**. Avoid staples unless your teacher tells you to use them.

SECTION 4
WRITING

In this section you will find the five steps of the writing process, with examples on how to brainstorm, write outlines, and draw word webs. There are also tips on research: getting started, supplies you may need, and how to take notes. Later in the section you'll find definitions and examples of many types of writing, including fiction, plays, poems, expository and persuasive writing, and letters. At the end of the section is a part on assessment and rubrics, so you can judge your own writing for yourself before you publish it.

THE FIVE-STEP WRITING PROCESS

The five steps to follow in the writing process are: **PREWRITING**, **DRAFTING**, **REVISING**, **PROOFREADING**, and **PUBLISHING**.

PREWRITING—Think
- Decide on a topic to write about.
- Consider who will read or listen to your written work.
- Brainstorm ideas about the subject.
- List places where you can research information.
- Do your research.

DRAFTING—Write
- Put the information you researched into your own words.
- Write sentences and paragraphs even if they are not perfect.
- Read what you have written and judge if it says what you mean.
- Show your writing to others and ask for suggestions.

REVISING—Make it Better
- Read what you have written again.
- Think about what others have said about your writing.
- Rearrange words or sentences.
- Take out or add parts to make your writing clearer or more complete.
- Replace overused or unclear words.
- Read your writing aloud to be sure it flows smoothly.

PROOFREADING—Make it Correct
- Be sure all sentences are complete.
- Correct spelling, capitalization, and punctuation.
- Change words that are not used correctly.
- Have someone check your work.
- Recopy your work correctly and neatly.

PUBLISHING—Share the Finished Product
- Read your writing aloud to a group.
- Create a book of your work.
- Send a copy to a friend or relative.
- Put your writing on display.
- Illustrate, perform, or set your creation to music.
- Congratulate yourself on a job well done!

GETTING STARTED

These five steps of the writing process are always flowing into and influencing one another without any clear line between them. Writing does not always happen in nice, neat steps. As the writer, you might get an idea for the conclusion while writing the introduction. The more you write and use this writing process, the easier it becomes. It's like riding a bike: when you first learn to ride, you are a little unsteady and unsure of yourself, but with practice, riding becomes automatic. The writing process becomes automatic too.

PREWRITING—THINK

The **prewriting step** in the process is the biggest part of writing your paper. It may seem like a lot to do at first, but once you're done prewriting, the hardest part is over.

Deciding on the Topic
The first step of prewriting is deciding on a topic. Think about the assignment: How long is it supposed to be? What type of paper is it supposed to be?

If your teacher gives you a general subject, try to narrow down a more specific topic from that subject. Make a **word web** of different topics and connected ideas. A web is a way to brainstorm ideas by putting them into a drawing. The circle in the middle shows the main topic. The other circles contain ideas about the main topic.

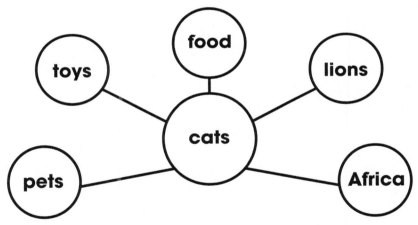

Use your word web to pick a topic that interests you. You will be spending time with this topic, and the more you like it, the more you will enjoy the research and writing you will do. You will also need to think about the **length** of your report. If your teacher wants one or two pages, you will need to have a narrower topic than if the assignment calls for five pages. You will also do a different amount of research depending on the length of the assigned report. Generally, a narrower topic will help you focus your research and make the writing of your paper easier. But be careful not to make your topic too narrow. If your topic is too specific, you may not be able to come up with enough information to write your report.

Look at the following topics. In this case, the teacher wanted the class to do a three to five page report of an aspect of the American Revolution.

The American Revolution (too broad)
Paul Revere's Light in the Old North Church (too specific)
Paul Revere (too broad)
Paul Revere's Role in the American Revolution (better)

If you have no topic, consult your **writer's journal**. Every writer should keep a notebook or journal. Write reactions to books, television, and movies. Write song lyrics you like. Write what you did that day. Write the names and brief descriptions of characters you dream up. Write settings that interest you. Write words you like and words you don't know. Just write. This journal is a great resource for your writing. Remember, the best source of ideas comes from you. When you're interested in your topic, you'll be more eager to write.

Decide on your Audience

Before you start writing or researching, decide on the audience for your paper. The audience is the group of people who will read or hear your work. If the project is a report for your class or a formal business letter, you will want to use **formal language**. However, if the project is a scary story or a friendly letter, you will probably use less formal language and your characters may use **informal language** in their dialogue. No matter what kind of writing you are doing, put your best work forward: use correct spelling and punctuation.

Also think about the purpose of your paper: will you **convince**, **inform**, or **entertain** your readers? When you convince, you change or encourage your reader's opinion in a persuasive essay. When you inform, you tell your reader all about a subject in an expository report. When you entertain, you tell your reader a story with fiction. Writing a persuasive essay is very different from writing a fable. Think about the words you will use to get your ideas across to your readers. Write down some ideas below your word web.

Brainstorm Ideas about the Subject

After you have decided on a topic and the audience of your writing, you are ready to **brainstorm**. When you brainstorm, you ask yourself questions about the topic you have chosen. Write down questions, phrases, words, or whatever comes to your mind when you think about your topic. Let your thoughts run free. Don't worry about organization, spelling, or punctuation—just write. Ask yourself: What do I know about this topic? What do I want to know about this topic? Below is an example of a brainstorming page. Use this as a model to begin your own brainstorming process.

Hurricanes

prevention?
time of year?
speed?
only over water?
where most frequent?
like a tornado?
conditions for movement over sea?
how different from typhoon?
why do they have names?

worst?
shelters?
last how long?
how to predict?
what kind of protection?
why?
what's the eye of the storm?
can I interview cousin Jackie from S.C.?

List places where you can research information

Once you've finished brainstorming, look over what you've written down and list places where you can research information on the topic. Even when you're writing a tall tale, it's a good idea to read a few tall tales yourself, just to be sure you know what is expected.

For science and history topics, use an **encyclopedia** first for an overview. Then check out an **almanac** for facts and statistics. An **atlas** may help, too. Finally, you'll want to search the **library** catalog for books and magazine articles you can use. For fiction, look up the genre, or the type of fiction, as a subject or keyword search.

There are many **resources** you can use when you write. Think about people you could interview, such as your grandparents or people in your community. Your own experience can be a great resource, too. Many authors say you should write about what you know from your own experience. This doesn't mean you can't write about aliens, dragons, or far away countries you've never been to, it just means that when you do write about those things, you should try to include ideas or problems that you have had in your own life.

Do your research

Whenever you do research, there are several steps to follow to be organized. Below is a list of supplies, ideas, and tips you can use to collect and organize your information easily.

Supplies

Use a **folder** to hold photocopies and handouts related to your report. It makes carrying all your information from school to home and from home to library easy and safe. Write your name and e-mail address or telephone number inside the folder in case you lose it.

Use **3 x 5 note cards** to write bibliography information about each source you use. Then when you write your bibliography, you can easily alphabetize the small cards. Use **4 x 6 note cards** for your notes. When you begin to write, you can lay these cards out and rearrange them as needed. This will help you organize your details before you start writing. When you research, keep a card or page in your notes set aside with the label, "dictionary words." Write down words that you don't know so you can look them up in the dictionary later. Be sure to keep **rubber bands** for each set of cards, and a **large envelope** for each set as well.

Finding Sources

Before you actually start doing your research and taking notes, you need to find sources. If your teacher would like you to use one encyclopedia, two books, two magazines, plus one additional source (almanac, atlas, biographical dictionary, etc.) you need to look at more than just one encyclopedia, more than two books, more than two magazines, etc. You want to find the information that will be the most informative on your topic. When you find a source, use your 3 x 5 note cards to keep track of the bibliography information.

- **Encyclopedia**
  Your library will likely have more than one set of encyclopedias. Use the encyclopedia's index volume and check two or three to compare the entries on your topic. It would take a long time to read all the entries, but if you read the first

and last paragraphs and the first sentence of some of the subsections of the entry, you will get a good idea of which encyclopedias will be most helpful to you.

- **Books**

When you are looking for your book sources—depending on your topic, you may find many books to choose from—check the table of contents and the index for your topic name. Again, decide which books have the most information on your topic and which will be most helpful to you when writing your report.

- **Magazines**

At the library, go to the *Reader's Guide* for magazines and copy down all the articles that have to do with your topic—there may be three or there may be ten. No matter how many, you should look up all the magazines that have information on your topic. After reading the first and last paragraphs and the first sentences of several paragraphs, decide if the article will help you. If you think you might use a particular magazine issue, write a check by the magazine information you wrote down. If you won't be using the article, cross out the information. Remember that having more than two "yes" checks is ok—you can decide which magazines will be most helpful when you do your actual note-taking later.

Skimming

Skimming is a technique you can use as you check out sources for your report. When you skim, you read quickly through the text, trying to understand the main points without slowing down for details. Skimming is an especially helpful reading technique to use when you are exploring a lengthy article or chapter for key pieces of information.

Taking Notes

After you have found your sources, you can begin taking notes. Use your brainstorming sheet. When you come to a fact or information that answers or relates to something you wrote down while brainstorming, write it down on a note card.

Note-Taking Tips

- Read the entire article or chapter before you start taking any notes—it's best to get an overview of what you are reading first to make sure you only take notes on what you need.
- Go back over the material and carefully select the information you want to include in your report. Stick with your chosen topic. Unless something seems very important, try to take notes only on information that answers the questions you wrote down during your brainstorming.
- First write the source information for your bibliography on a 3 x 5 card. Number this card (1, 2, 3). Then on a 4 x 6 card, write the question from the brainstorming sheet and the information from the source that answers that question. Write the number of the source at the top of the card.
- When you come to a fact or an idea you want to record, close the book. Think about what you've been reading, and then write the fact down in your own words. When you avoid copying right out of the book, it helps you put things in your own words and avoid plagiarizing. (See more about **Avoiding Plagiarism** in **Section 6—Research**.)

- Facts, measurements, dates, or other statistics may be copied directly. This information belongs to everyone. Just be sure to include these facts in sentences with your own words.
- If you find a whole paragraph you would like to take notes on, paraphrase and summarize the paragraph into just three sentences that condense the most important information.
- If you want to use the author's words (you may want to do this if the author is expressing an opinion), copy the words down exactly and put quotation marks around them so you won't forget that it is a quote. Then write the page number where the quote is found.

Research with Caution

When you research, be aware of the dates on your sources. You should try to use books and magazines that are not more than five years old. With some topics, such as animals, you do not need to be as careful. A book published in 1990 on the polar bear will probably have information that is just as good as a book published in 2004.

However, if you are researching any scientific, geographic, or current topic where new information is available constantly, it is best that your sources be as current as possible. In fact, magazines and the latest almanac will very likely be your best sources.

You might also find conflicting facts in the sources you use. Dates of events, especially, may be different. Do not worry about this. If you can, compare more than two sources to see if a third can help you clarify a fact.

Fact or Opinion?

In your research, you'll come across facts and opinions. It is important to know the difference so you can collect accurate information. A **fact** is a statement that is accurate. It has truth. It can be checked and supported by other facts. An **opinion** is a belief. It is someone's thought or feeling about a subject. It may or may not be true. There are certain words that may signal an opinion: *believe, feel, think, better,* or *even more.*

> Scientists believe more money should be spent in studying space.
> Scientists have been studying problems in space.

In the first sentence, the words *believe* and *more* are both used. This statement is the opinion of the scientists. The second statement is a fact. The scientists are studying space.

DRAFTING—WRITE

Now it is time to put the information you researched into your own words. When you have all your note cards together and all your research is done, you are ready to begin the **drafting** process. The first thing you should do is to write an outline.

Organizing an Outline

An **outline** lists the information you have gathered in the order you will write it in your paper. An outline has topics (I, II, III, IV), subtopics (A, B, C), and details (1, 2, 3).

Think of your outline as a map—this map will guide you from the beginning of your report to the end. Pretend that you are explaining your topic to a friend. What would you explain first? Second? Third? This will help you order your main ideas for the outline.

The outline, like your paper, should have a beginning, a middle, and an end. At the **beginning**, you introduce the topic and explain what you will be talking about in your report. The **middle** of the report is called the body. Here you give the reader all the details. The **end** is called the conclusion. In your conclusion, you can sum up or repeat the main idea, give your personal opinion on the topic, or give a prediction about what will happen in the future. You should only do this last type of conclusion if your topic is a current event or scientific discovery.

First, group your note cards into three sections: beginning, middle, and end. All the cards in one section should relate to the same general subtopic. Next, organize the middle part. Decide if you will use a chronological pattern (arranging the cards according to what happened in time). If your report topic is more scientific, order the cards from general facts to specific facts. If you have three or four strong subtopics, organize the cards into these groups.

Once you have your cards organized, you can write your outline. Include only the key points on the outline. Don't bother to write out the facts and details; simply list the topics or questions, so you'll know what to write next.

Outline: Life in France
- I.   Introduction to Life in France
- II.   Daily Activities
  - A. School
  - B. Entertainment
    - 1. art
    - 2. movies
- III. Foods
  - A. Cheeses and Appetizers
    - 1. Escargot
    - 2. Foie Gras
  - B. Main dishes
  - C. Desserts

IV.   Going to Paris
        A. Eiffel Tower
        B. Louvre Museum
        C. Arch de Triumph
V.   Conclusion

Write sentences and paragraphs even if they are not perfect. When your outline is complete, you are ready to start writing your first draft.

Writing a Paragraph

A **paragraph** is a group of sentences that belong together. When you begin a new idea or paragraph, start on a new line and indent the first word several spaces from the left margin. A **paper** is a group of paragraphs about one topic. Sometimes a paper is so short that it is only one paragraph long. No matter how many paragraphs you write, you develop them in the same way unless you are writing a dialogue in a story. Remember, all sentences in the paragraph have a close relationship to each other.

First, develop your main idea according to a specific order. Your sentences may be written according to time, space, or order of importance. Words used to show order include: *first, last, second, next, finally, then, tomorrow, before, after, least, smallest,* or *most important.*

A paragraph starts with an introductory sentence that tells the main idea. Supporting sentences add details. Once you know your purpose and order, write smooth-flowing, supporting sentences. They give details, reasons, examples, or likenesses and/or differences. The concluding paragraph of a paper usually draws together the supporting details and restates the main idea.

Details help the reader form a clearer picture. See how these details help you picture Robin's skateboard:

> Robin enjoys her new skateboard.
> Robin enjoys her shiny, red skateboard with the turned-up, pointed front.

Reasons are provided when the writer wants to persuade the reader. Sometimes writers show how their topic is like something the reader knows. Vocabulary used to show likenesses includes *also, just as, in the same manner, resembles,* and *similarly.* To develop a paragraph that shows differences, you might include words like *by contrast, on the other hand, unlike, on the contrary,* and *but.*

Skip every other line as you write or double-space your typed paper so that there will plenty of room around the text for you to add comments, suggestions, and new sentences. Read what you have written and judge if it says what you mean. Write through your whole outline. When you've finished this first draft, read it carefully.

Staying on Topic

Staying on topic is very important to your writing. As you read your writing, ask yourself: What is the main idea of this paragraph? Do these sentences give reasons, examples, details, or facts that support the main idea of the paragraph? Remember the *W*s of

writing as you read: **who**, **what**, **where**, **when**, **why**, and **how**. Do your paragraphs and sentences answer these questions? Think of your paper as a picture: each sentence is a detail and each paragraph is a group of details. Together these details make up a larger image.

Show your draft to others and ask for suggestions.

After you have read through your draft once, give it to a friend, brother, sister, or parent to read. Have him or her read only for the text—don't worry about punctuation, spelling, or other errors at this time. Have your reader ask the same questions you asked yourself: What is the main idea of this paragraph? Do these sentences give reasons, examples, details, or facts that directly relate to the main idea of the paragraph? Do the paragraphs and sentences answer the questions who, what, where, when, why, and how? Ask what your reader thinks you can do to improve the contents of your paper.

REVISING—MAKE IT BETTER

Re-Read What You Have Written
Do your math homework, play a game, take a walk, or wait until the next morning before you read your paper again. Then ask yourself the same questions. What can you do to make the contents better? Think about what others have said about your draft. Make a list of comments and suggestions your readers—and you—have thought of.

Rearrange
Start with your introduction and work through the paper, writing notes, rearranging words and sentences, and writing new sentences between the lines and in the margins. You may discover that you are missing a key fact or detail. Go back to your sources and notes if necessary to fill the gap in your research.

Replace Overused or Unclear Words
Part of improving the content of your paper is making sure every word you use means what you want it to mean. As you review your draft, use a thesaurus to look up synonyms for overused words. Replace words that confuse your readers. Read each sentence and ask yourself: what is the point I am trying to make? Condense each sentence to its main idea. Replace or remove confusing or extra words.

Read your Writing Aloud to Be Sure it Flows Smoothly
After you've made so many changes, you'll need to reread the whole paper to make sure it still flows and makes sense. This time, read it aloud. Reading aloud helps you to go slower. You'll catch more mistakes this way.

Prepare your Bibliography
At the end of a research report, you must include a bibliography to give credit to your sources. A bibliography is an alphabetical listing, by author, of the sources you used for information. Books, magazines, encyclopedias, and other sources each have their own bibliographical form.

Book:
Last Name, First Name of Author. *The Title in Italics*. Place of Publication: Publisher, date of publication.
> Sail, T.H. *The Story of Boats*. Boatweave, New Jersey: Wave Press, 1989.

Magazine:
Last Name, First Name of Author. "Title of Article in Quotation Marks," <u>Title of Magazine Underlined</u> (Date of issue in parenthesis), pages.

> Rogers, William. "How to Train your Parakeet," <u>Pet Magazine</u> (April 7, 1989), 85-87.

Encyclopedia:
Last Name, First Name of Author if Given. "Title of Article in Quotation Marks," <u>Title of Encyclopedia Underlined</u>. Year. Volume Number, pages.
> "Pirates," <u>Encyclopedia of History</u>. 1987. Volume 18, pp. 188-191.

Internet:
Last Name, First Name of Author if Given. "Article Title in Quotation Marks," Web site address. Date revised or updated.

Needlman, Robert. "Adolescent Stress," **http://www.drspock.com/article**. June, 2003.

It is a good idea to print all Internet sources, so you will have the content and the address at the top of the page.

Bibliography Note Cards
Use the following cards as a reference to help you prepare your bibliography 3 x 5 cards during research.

Book Bibliography Card

Author: _____

Title: _____

Place of Publication: _____

Publisher: _____

Copyright Date: _____ Pages: _____

Encyclopedia Bibliography Card

Author (if given): _____

Title of Article: _____

Name of Encyclopedia: _____

Copyright Date: _____ Volume: _____

Pages: _____

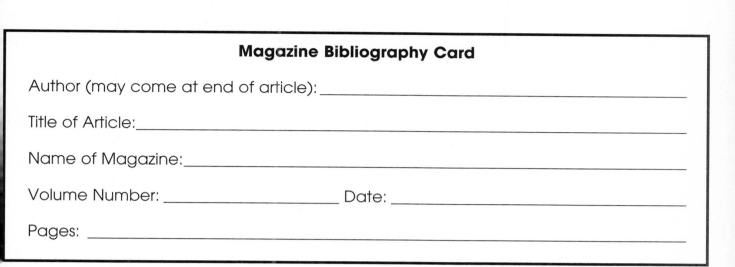

Magazine Bibliography Card

Author (may come at end of article): _____

Title of Article: _____

Name of Magazine: _____

Volume Number: _____ Date: _____

Pages: _____

Internet Bibliography Card

Author: _____

Title of Article: _____

Full Web site address: http://www. _____

Date page was last revised: _____

PROOFREADING—MAKE IT CORRECT

Be Sure All Sentences Are Complete
Take another break from your paper. When you come back to it, you'll be ready to start proofreading it. Proofreading is different from revising. When you revise, you work on the quality of the content. When you proofread, you work on the correctness of spelling, punctuation, and word usage.

Start by rereading each sentence. Make sure it is a complete sentence and not a fragment. Also review your sentences to make sure they are not too long. Shorten run-on sentences by removing extra words or adding punctuation.

Correct Spelling, Capitalization, and Punctuation
Carefully read your work and correct spelling, capitalization, and punctuation errors. Does every sentence start with a capital letter? Does each sentence have the proper commas and end punctuation? Pay special attention to dialogue and sentences that use quotation marks. For help with this, use **Section 3: Mechanics**.

Check for Correct Word Usage
Homophones and words with multiple meanings can confuse you. Part of checking spelling is making sure that you used the proper spelling of words like *there, they're,* and *their,* or *scent, cent,* and *sent.* Change contractions to two words. If you used a word and you're not sure if you used it correctly, take the time to look it up in the dictionary. Make sure you used nouns as nouns and verbs as verbs—changing a word's part of speech can make it meaningless or confusing to the reader.

Proofreading Tips
Sometimes you think you wrote one thing but actually you did not. This makes it difficult for you to find mistakes in your own writing. You read what you meant to say rather than the actual words on the page. It helps to put the writing away overnight. This gives your brain time to forget what you wrote. Later, you will be able to see the words that are actually on the page. It helps to read your work aloud, word for word. Listen to see whether it makes sense. Try to identify missing or extra words. Read your work again, silently. Look carefully for mistakes in punctuation, spelling, and grammar. Find punctuation mistakes by reading the sentences aloud and backwards. Start with the last sentence, then read the next-to-last sentences, and so on. If what you read doesn't sound like a sentence, check the punctuation.

Proofread for mistakes in spelling, punctuation, capitalization, and verb usage. It is best to check your work for no more than two items at a time. Here's a proofreading checklist.

Proofreading Checklist
    I. Mechanics
        A. Spelling
            1. Use homophones correctly.
            2. Change contractions to two words.
        B. Capitalization
            1. Start all sentences with a capital letter including sentences inside dialogue.

2. Capitalize specific names of people, places, and things.
C. Punctuation
   1. Punctuate the end of each sentence properly.
   2. Place commas in compound sentences and in items listed in a series.
   3. Punctuate dialogue or conversation with quotation marks and commas.

II. Usage
   A. Check your use of commonly misused words.
   B. Check for correct subject/verb agreement.

III. Read your writing to make sure the meaning is clear and complete.

Once you've made all your changes, have a friend read it for punctuation, spelling, and word usage errors you may have missed.

Proofreading Symbols

Symbol	Meaning	Example
#	new paragraph	# Many children have lived in the White House.
≡	capital letter	Theodore roosevelt's family may have been the most spirited bunch.
/	lowercase letter	His son, Quentin, once snuck a Pony inside!
^	insert	Why did Quentin do that? He wanted to cheer up his brother.
℘	delete (take out)	Theodore Roosevelt had had six children.
⊙	add a period	Archie and Quentin were the youngest ⊙
˅	add an apostrophe	Alice was Theodore Roosevelt's oldest child.
⌃	add a comma	Some people thought Alice was too wild, and they criticized Roosevelt.
˅˅	add quotation marks	He responded, I can be president, or I can supervise Alice. Nobody could do both.

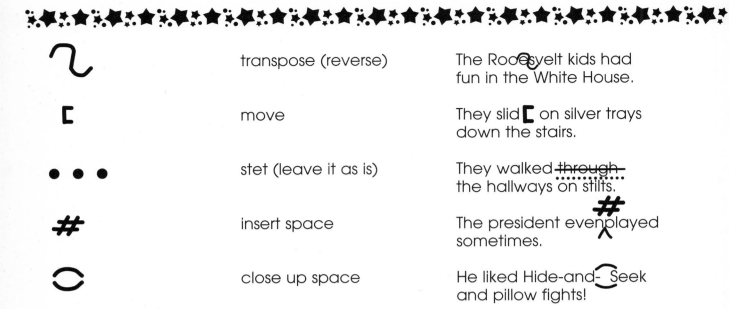

	transpose (reverse)	The Roosevelt kids had fun in the White House.
	move	They slid **⊏** on silver trays down the stairs.
• • •	stet (leave it as is)	They walked ~~through~~ the hallways on stilts.
#	insert space	The president even played sometimes.
⊃⊂	close up space	He liked Hide-and-Seek and pillow fights!

Write Final Copy

After you've finished revising and proofreading, you're ready to rewrite a fresh, error-free copy with all the changes you've made. Use your best penmanship or type carefully. Even if the content is a masterpiece, your readers will notice misspellings and punctuation mistakes. Put the pages in a folder or notebook for safekeeping, so they won't be folded, bent, or creased. Watch out for bad weather and the cafeteria, too. Water, mud, food, and pets are a final copy's worst enemies!

PUBLISHING—SHARE THE FINISHED PRODUCT

Now that you've got a finished product, share it! Here are some ideas for getting your writing out into the world.

Group Reading
Start an Author's Group with your friends or classmates. Get together and take turns reading your work. Then discuss each piece. Set ground rules for discussion, such as a list of questions you will ask every author, and agree to respect one another's work by taking it seriously. Don't forget to bring snacks to share!

Create a Book
Use a three-hole punch and ribbon or twist-ties to bind your pages together. You can also have your work professionally bound at a copy center. Some art supply stores have blank, pre-bound books that you can fill in for yourself. You can handwrite in your text or cut your typed pages to fit. Use illustrations, computer art and graphics, or stickers to decorate the book.

Send a Copy to a Friend or Relative
Believe it or not, your friends and relatives would love to see your creativity. You may be surprised the next time you visit to see your creation on someone's coffee table or refrigerator! Books make great gifts, too. You can write special stories for birthdays or anniversaries.

Put Your Writing on Display
Ask your librarian if you can display your work in the juvenile or young adult section of the local library. You could ask your school librarian, too. Who knows how many other people will follow your example? Putting your work on display is a great way to encourage other writers and to help writers get new ideas for their future projects.

Illustrate, Perform, or Set Your Creation to Music
If you've written a play, it's time to perform it! Remember that the most important part of putting on a play is the acting. It doesn't matter if you don't have all the props, or if you don't have a real theater in which to perform. Just do your best! The audience will appreciate your effort—and your great story!

Congratulate Yourself!
Take the time to think about your writing. What is your favorite part of the piece? What do you wish you had done differently? What was the hardest part of the process? Write down your reflections in your writer's journal. Your ideas will help you when it's time to write again!

GENRES

A **genre** is a particular type of category. In literature, there are many categories, or genres, of fiction. These include science fiction, tall tales, and mysteries, just to name a few. There are non-fiction genres, too: biography, poetry, persuasive essays, and expository reports.

FICTION WRITING

Fiction is not true. Stories, poems, plays, myths, fables, mysteries, science fiction, historical fiction, and realistic fiction are genres of fiction. Even though each type of fiction has different elements, they are all types of stories. Every story needs a problem to solve (the plot), a setting, and interesting characters. It should also have a beginning, a middle, and an end. Here are some important parts of stories.

Characters
The most important part of many stories is the **characters**. The reader has to understand and care about the characters if the story is going to be successful. The author develops characters in three ways: by what he or she shows about the character, by what the character says, and by what the character does. Good writers show; they don't tell. See the difference below between telling what a character is like and showing what a character is like.

How a character...	Telling	Showing
Looked:	He was strong.	Muscles bulged under his shirt.
Felt:	He felt sad.	A dark cloud seemed to settle over him.
Acted	She was friendly.	She smiled and waved at everyone.
Talked	She said a car was coming.	She screamed, "Watch out for the car!"

Write so your reader knows what the characters look like, say, do, think, and feel. The best way to do this is to include **sensory details** that draw upon any of the five senses—**sight**, **sound**, **smell**, **touch**, and even **taste**. Help the reader experience the situation just as the character did. Bring your characters to life. "Jill was sad as she watched Amy leave" is not as descriptive as "Jill sighed heavily as her best friend disappeared into the distance. Amy was headed toward a new town and a new life—without Jill."

Setting
The **setting** defines the space in which the story takes place. Think of the setting not just as the **where**, but also the **when**. Depending on the type of fiction you are writing, your story may take place in the past, present, or future. It may also take place underwater, in space, or in China. Describe the setting when it will make the most impact in the story. Use one of the first paragraphs of your story to define your space. Or tell the reader where the story takes place, but wait until later in the story to reveal your time. Deciding how and when to explain the setting can build mystery and suspense.

Plot

What happens in a story is the **plot**, or plan. The plot introduces, builds, and finally solves a problem. At the beginning of the story, the author introduces the characters and the setting. The writer also introduces a **problem**. Through the middle of the story, the characters are developed as they deal with the problem. Then, towards the end, the **climax** occurs. The climax is the answer or solution to the problem and it should be the height of the action. The end resolves any minor details and wraps up the action. The **solution** may be that there is no solution, but at least the character or characters have gained a new insight about the situation.

The plot is the heart of the story. Think of an interesting or funny problem, then think of a solution. Don't forget to explain and develop the events or episodes of the story in the proper sequence. You may tell the story chronologically from start to finish. You may decide to tell the story backwards. Be creative and decide what will work best in the story: it will help to show the reader a clear connection between the problem, the main character, and the character's feelings.

Theme

The **theme** of a story is the main point the writer wants to get across. If the story is about a struggle two friends go through, then the theme is probably the importance of friendship. If something bad happens and the main character has to get through it, then the theme could be perseverance or courage. Answer the following questions to strengthen your theme.

> What do you want your readers to think about most when they finish your story? Are the characters or the events in the plot more important to your message? What sentences, dialogue, or descriptions can you improve to make your message clearer?

Tone

The **tone** of the story is the mood that it creates. Are the characters depressed? Is the setting peaceful? The tone of the story is important to getting the theme across. Again, think about how you want your readers to feel as they read the story. If the story is about the main character's triumph, then the tone will probably be happy and light. If the main character's dog dies, then the tone will probably be depressed and sad.

The Narrator: First, Second, or Third Person

You can choose one of three plans for telling the actual story. **First person** means that the main character tells the story. He or she will talk about things from his or her point of view and use the pronoun *I* when he or she explains how he or she feels.

Second person is not very common, but it can be really creative. Second person is being spoken to. In this case, the narrator will be telling the story of what a character is doing to that character, using the pronoun *you*: "You walked out onto the sidewalk and breathed in the cool spring air. The sight of budding trees and the smell of daffodils delighted your senses."

Third person is probably the most common. Third person is being spoken about. When

you write a report, you should always use the third person. You should avoid putting the word *I* in a report because you are reporting facts, not your opinion. The third person pronouns are *he, she, it,* and *they.* The narrator will tell about the characters.

You may want to try two different narrators. Let a main character tell part of the story, and then switch back to third person. Only do this if you can make an obvious break between the sections: you don't want to confuse your reader—or yourself!

Point of View

When you choose a narrator, you are also choosing the **point of view**. The point of view describes who tells the story. It is the narrator's version of the events that we will read throughout the story. This is why it works well sometimes to switch narrators. The new narrator gives the readers a new point of view on something they've already heard about from the original narrator's perspective.

Most authors do not show things from their villains' points of view. They want their readers to connect with the heroes of the story, so they show events from a hero's point of view.

Dialogue

You can record a conversation between characters using **dialogue**, but you can also develop action. Just imagine: two characters are wandering through an abandoned house in the dark without flashlights:

> "Did you hear something?" Holly breathed. She held Adam's arm tighter.
> Almost immediately Adam whispered, "What was that?"
> "There's a light...under that door," Holly replied, gesturing towards the end of the hall with her head. "What should we do?"

Here the dialogue explains what is happening without the author just telling us, adding suspense to the scene.

A **direct quotation** is the use of someone's exact words. It is always set off with quotation marks. An **indirect quotation** is the writer's description of someone else's words. It does not require quotation marks.

> direct: Brent said, "Ben is bringing the dog to the vet."
> indirect: Brent said that Ben is bringing the dog to the vet.

Foreshadowing

Foreshadowing lets the writer clue the reader in on events that will happen later in the story. The author can insert little comments with words like *if only, maybe if,* or *perhaps that's why.* These comments lead the reader to think about the possible future event. They can reduce the shock of the climax of the story. For example:

> If only Celia had listened to her mother's advice that morning.
> Perhaps that's why she didn't hear our shouts from the opposite corner.

REALISTIC FICTION

Unlike all the types of fiction above, **realistic fiction** could actually happen. It may even be based on actual events. Realistic fiction has human characters living the present that deal with everyday problems and come up with everyday solutions. The themes of realistic fiction are things we all deal with: friendships, families, loss, courage, perseverance, and growing up. Here's an example:

Emily's Play

Emily knew that this was her big chance. She stepped out onto the stage and drew in all that lay before her: the audience waiting anxiously in the half-light, her friends standing on their masking-tape marks in full costume, their shiny faces beaded with makeup. She saw her older brother close one eye ever so quickly—their special signal. She strode over to him. Slowly her lips curled up in a grin, as she said her very first line, "What a fine day for a picnic, Mr. McGillicutty."

Emily was an actress.

"Emily, you were amazing! I can't believe it!"

"Wow, what a compliment. Did you really think I would mess up my big chance?"

"Of course I did," Drew said with a twinkle in his eye. He winked.

Emily rolled her eyes. "Ha ha, Drew. You're hilarious."

Drew caught Emily in his big-brother grip and held her tight. "You were great, Em," he said seriously.

Emily pushed him away and batted at something in her eye. They grinned at each other.

Corrie, Sandra, and David rushed up to congratulate her, throwing big bouquets of daisies and carnations into Emily's arms as they kissed her cheeks and hugged her tightly. Corrie and Sandra's eyes met. They clasped hands and started dancing around in a circle, cheering, "Emily! Emily!"

Historical Fiction

Historical fiction is a lot like realistic fiction: it deals with real people and their real problems. The difference is that historical fiction is set in an historical period during an historical event. Karen Hesse's book *Out of the Dust* is a good example of historical fiction. In it, a girl tells the story of her life during the Great Depression. She explains what it was like to live during a time when people had little money because of the stock market crash. She talks about school, farm life, and her troubles, so the reader can understand what it was like to live during that period of American history.

Historical Fiction Builders

Who is the main character?
Who's telling the story?

During which historic time period does the character live?
What is the world like during this time? (Think about clothes, homes, everyday life, roles of men and women, and school.)

Which events in the plot will be from history and which will be from fiction?
What problems does the main character face?

Could this story happen today?

Mystery
Missing people, dark shadows, mysterious strangers, footsteps in the night, strange occurrences—all of these mixed together make for a good mystery story. In addition to these characteristics, there are several other factors that make a story into a mystery. The more of the following ingredients a mystery has, the better the story is likely to be:

Suspense
This is the nervous feeling you get while reading that something is going to happen, but you don't know what it is or when it will happen. Build suspense using sensory descriptions and revealing key facts slowly or unexpectedly.

Clues
A good mystery should have clues so that the reader can follow the action and try to figure out the answer before the characters figure it out in the story.

False leads
A lead is information that can be of possible use to you in a search. False leads will keep the reader wandering off the path to the real answers. False leads will keep the reader in suspense as he or she reads.

Answer these questions to write your own mystery:

Mystery Builders
Who is the detective/mystery solver?
What does (name) look like?
What is (name) like?

Who are the detective's assistants, if any?
Who are the mysterious characters (also called suspects)?

List some clues that help solve the mystery.

List any false leads in the story.

How is the mystery solved?

FANTASY

Fantasy stories could never be real. They include fantastic characters like witches, dragons, talking animals, and unicorns. Fantasies often take place in imaginary settings. Fairy tales, fables, tall tales, and science fiction are all types of fantasy writing.

Fairy Tales

We all know **fairy tales** from our childhood. Stories like *Snow White, Hansel and Gretel,* and *The Little Mermaid* are well-known fairy tales. Fairy tales are fantasy stories, because most of them have some fantastic characters or settings. Gingerbread houses, mermaids, witches, and fairies inhabit this type of fiction. Here's an example:

Cora and the Giant

Once upon a time, in a kingdom far, far away, there lived a beautiful princess named Cora. Cora never listened to what her father said, and she liked to take long walks outside the palace walls every afternoon.

One day Cora was out strolling when she heard the silver trumpets ringing their call for supper. She hadn't realized that it was getting so late, but sure enough the west was a jumble of red, orange, and pink and above her the sky was growing dark. But Cora didn't feel like going in just yet. She turned away from the castle and strode off into the darkening woods.

Almost immediately she came upon a glistening pond. Although it was growing dark, the water was crystal clear, and it seemed to sparkle like the moon in the dusk. Cora was suddenly aware of her thirst. She bent down slowly, careful not to get her dress dirty, and cupped her hands under the icy water.

With a startling whoosh of air and a cannon ball of a splash, Cora sprang back from the pond. Her startled eyes beheld a giant standing before her. He had risen eight feet out of the water and stood glowering at her, droplets dripping down from his bald green head past his deep purple eyes to his long, frowning face. Cora stared in amazement.

Fable

A fable is an old type of story. It dates back to Ancient Greece. Thinkers and writers like Socrates and Aesop used fables to get across a specific message or moral to their listeners and readers. A **fable** is a simple story with an important message, or moral, for the reader. In Aesop's fable, *The Tortoise and the Hare*, the turtle, which is much slower, wins the race because the much faster rabbit thinks he can't lose and takes unnecessary breaks. The moral of the story is that skill alone does not lead to success in life. The turtle proved that you need dedication and perseverance to succeed.

Tall Tales

Tall tales were especially popular in America when the first settlers started moving west. **Tall tales** are "tall" because they are exaggerated, incredible, and not likely to be true. They exaggerate a character's size or what he or she can do. Paul Bunyan, John Henry, Pecos Bill, and Casey Jones are popular characters from tall tales. Here's an example:

The Giant From Mars

Years ago when the world was young, a giant came down from Mars. He was fifteen miles tall and not very smart. When he lay down, he made the English Channel. He took his bath in the Indian Ocean, and he went swimming in the Atlantic Ocean. After his swim, when he put his hand on land, he made the Great Lakes. When he sat down to eat lunch, he made the Grand Canyon. Then he amused himself by making sand castles. These sand castles became the Great Smoky Mountains. After a while, he went back for another swim. This time, he made all of the valleys, and he broke a dam, which let the ice from the Arctic into the United States. This made all of our glaciers.

Science Fiction

Science fiction is a type of fantasy that uses scientific ideas and a setting controlled by scientific possibilities. Time travel, space travel, the development of new species of animals, and living in cities underwater are all science fiction topics, because they rely on scientific ideas and details. Futuristic technology is very important to science fiction.

Science Fiction Builders

Who is the main character?
Does he or she have special powers or abilities?
What is his or her goal or purpose?
How does the main character set about achieving goals or solving problems?
What obstacles does the character face?

Where and when does the story take place?

Who are the other characters?
Who's telling the story?

Describe any science-related elements of the story.
What is the climax or most exciting moment of the story?

PLAYS

A **play** is a type of fiction written just for actors who will tell the story with their words and actions on a **stage**. A play is told in **acts** and **scenes**. Plays can have one to five acts. The writer splits up the action so that it will fit into these acts. A scene takes place in one location only. Characters can come and go from that scene, but the place stays the same.

The **setting** of the play should be simple—there should only be a few different locations. The writer should describe the sets—where the scenes take place—at the beginning of the scene. A set can be as simple as a desk and chair to show that the characters are in an office. It can also have fancy background paintings that show a city skyline, or a whole set of bedroom furniture. As the writer you can make the sets as simple or as involved as you want. Remember that the characters have to explain and show everything to the audience. Include lines to help the viewer understand where the characters are: Whose house is it? Whose office is it? What building is it? What city does the story take place in?

The **characters** are the most important part of a play because they tell the whole story. The writer develops the plot using dialogue and monologue. **Dialogue** is conversation between characters. A **monologue** is a speech by one character. The audience or other characters may listen to the monologue. Monologues are a good way of giving the audience information that none of the other characters knows. It's a good way to build suspense in a mystery.

Give the character **stage directions**, too. Stage directions tell the character where to move and how to act while reading his or her dialogue. If the character has to hug her mother while saying a certain line, be sure to include that as a stage direction.

Play Builders
Title
Theme
Genre: Is the play a comedy, drama, or mystery? Is it historical, realistic, or fantastic?

Main character
Main character's personality

Another main character
This character's personality
Supporting characters

Setting (time and place)
General Plot

POEMS

A writer writes a poem to tell something or show something, just like a story. Poetry expresses the imagination with an arrangement of words and phrases. Usually, poetry is not written in complete sentences. It is just a different form of story telling. It has character, theme, tone, point of view, and description just like a story. A poem can be written in several different forms. Some are stricter than others.

Limerick
A **limerick** is supposed to be funny, silly, and ridiculous. Limericks consist of five lines. The first, second, and fifth lines rhyme with one another and have three beats. The third and fourth lines also rhyme with one another and have two beats.

> There was a young fellow named Fisher,
> Who was fishing for fish in a fissure.
>> Then a cod with a grin
>> Pulled the fisherman in. . .
> Now they're fishing the fissure for Fisher.

Concrete Poetry
Concrete poetry is written about a picture of an object, such as a ball, truck, flower, or even fingers. The object becomes part of the poem and the words of the poem are arranged around or within the object. The arrangement of the words and the object chosen should express the feeling of the poem.

Cinquain
A **cinquain** is based on a five-line pattern. Although there are a number of different patterns, the most often used is 1-2-3-4-1. The first line has one word, the second has two, the third has three, the fourth has four, and the fifth has one. Each line has a purpose:

Line 1 states the theme of the poem.
Line 2 describes the theme of the poem.
Line 3 provides an action for the theme.
Line 4 gives a feeling of the theme.
Line 5 states another word for the theme.

> Rain
> soft drizzle
> falls on plants
> quiet splashes of water
> Growth.

Haiku

Haiku is one of the oldest forms of Japanese poetry. Unlike cinquains, which are patterns of words, haiku is a pattern of syllables. Haiku consists of three lines of seventeen syllables total. Five syllables are in the first line, seven are in the second line, and five are in the third line. The most important thing about haiku is the feeling of the poem. Themes in haiku are usually beauty and nature.

Light dance on water
hopping from ripple to wave
Flickering light fades.

Free verse

Free verse is just that: free. A free verse poem has no set rhyme scheme, no specific number of lines, and it can be about anything you want to write about.

Indian Summer day
deep blue sky far away and laughing
Trees burn in autumn colors—see the smoke rise as wispy cloud
Miles and miles above,
Geese
in their autumn flock's "V"
swim through the sky.

NON-FICTION WRITING

Biography

A **biography** is the story of a person's life not written by that person. You may think of biographies as only being about people who lived hundreds of years ago, but biographies are written about celebrities in sports, movies, and politics every day. Check out the biography section of the library to find hundreds of biographies about all kinds of people. To write a biography, it is a good idea to use a few biographies as sources. Compare the facts and ideas in each book. Collect research for a biography just as you would for an expository report.

Biography Builders

Who is the biography about?
When did (or does) this person live?
What was (is) this person famous for?

Where and when was this person born?
What was his or her education like?
What dreams did he or she have while growing up?
What would you consider one turning point in this person's life?

Who were other people who helped this person achieve his or her goals?
Do you feel this person struggled much to reach his or her goals? Why or why not?
What affect has this person had on your life? Why did you want to write this biography?

Autobiography

An **autobiography** is the story of the writer's life. You can only write your own autobiography. *Auto* is a Greek root that means "self." Make a list of important events and people in your life. Decide on a theme and a tone for your autobiography. What do you want your readers to know about your life? Decide what message you would like to give your readers. You can write your autobiography in the first person.

Expository Reports

Expository reports give information about a subject using description, facts, or examples. Reports inform and explain. In a report that informs, the writer gives information about a topic. In a report that explains, the writer explains how to do something. Once you have chosen a topic and decided whether you need to inform or explain, make a **K-W-L chart**.

K- What I Know	W- What I Want to Know	L- What I Have Learned

First, list all the things you know about your topic in the K column. Next, list all the questions you have about your topic under the W column. Then, research the topic. List the most important things you learned about your topic in the L column. This chart is a more organized form of your brainstorming sheet. Use either a brainstorming sheet or a K-W-L chart to gather research.

Organization

The most important part of writing an expository report is organizing your information. You want your facts and details to flow in such a way that they make sense and are of interest to the reader. Here are some choices:

- **Chronological order**

Organize the facts in order of chronological time if you are writing about something that happened over time, such as a war, a famous person's life, the life cycle of an animal, or changes in climate. You will describe the events in the order they happened.

- **Order of importance**

This is a good approach if you are writing about the causes of something (such as allergies), the use of something (such as gold), or a scientist's inventions. Start with the most important item and proceed to the least important items.

- **Problem-cause-solution**

This approach is helpful for topics such as ways to avoid skin cancer, better ways to distribute the world's food, ways to save energy, or ways to solve another problem. **Describe** the problem, **explain** the cause, and **conclude** with the solution.

Here is an example of an expository report. This report explains the operation of the Pony Express to the reader. It is organized using problem-cause-solution, and by order of importance. The author introduces the problem (slow mail) and its cause (the long distance over which mail must travel) in the first few sentences. Then the author explains a solution (the Pony Express). After the introduction, the author organizes the report by order of importance.

The Pony Express

Before 1860, the mail routes from the Eastern United States to California were not very reliable. There wasn't an official mail service. Mail went on ships bound for Panama, South America. Then it was carried across tropical jungles in order to be reloaded on ships heading for the west coast. The route took about twenty-two days. Mail also went on an overland stagecoach route that took about twenty-five days. William H. Russell of the freighting firm Russell, Majors, and Waddell, believed mail should have its own service that could guarantee delivery. He developed the Pony Express and boasted that it could get mail from St. Joseph, Missouri, to Sacramento, California, faster than any other company. He hoped that the Pony Express would solve the mail delivery problem until the telegraph lines could be completed.

With the Pony Express, the mail took about ten days to cover 1,996 miles. It was carried by one of about 120 riders, who would gallop up to a relay station along the route, throw his mail pouch onto a waiting horse, and be off, all within two minutes. These relay stations were about ten miles apart and were usually located at a stream or spring. The record run over the whole line was made carrying President Abraham Lincoln's Inaugural Address in seven days and seventeen hours.

Pony Express riders were selected from the most hardy and courageous of the frontiersmen. They had to be lightweight and tough enough to ride through storms, over snowcapped mountains, across burning deserts, and through streams. They agreed not to use profane language, not to get drunk, not to gamble, not to treat animals cruelly, and not to do anything that was incompatible with the conduct of a gentleman. Each rider was given a small Bible to carry among his belongings.

PERSUASIVE ESSAY

When you write an essay, you are expressing your thoughts and opinions about a topic. In a **persuasive essay**, you encourage your readers to think the same things that you do. A persuasive essay uses argument to encourage a reader to accept the author's opinions.

First, decide what you want to talk someone into doing or believing. Narrow your topic just as you would for an expository report. Decide on an audience. Gather evidence to support your belief, or gather evidence and then formulate an opinion. Evidence includes facts and information. Learn as much as you can about your subject to make a convincing argument. Research articles, interview people, or write for information to gather evidence. Determine why you believe what you do about your subject. Remember to take notes and keep a bibliography of your sources as part of the prewriting process.

When you are ready to write your outline, you are ready to organize your arguments. The **introduction** needs to present your position with a strong statement about your stand on the issue. Organize your arguments from strongest to weakest. The strongest arguments are the ones that have the most support from your research. The weakest arguments have the least support. As you write each paragraph, start with a topic sentence that introduces the new argument. Then support that argument with facts and details. The **body** of the composition simply supports your position with clear reasons, facts, and examples as to why you believe as you do. Write a **conclusion** and include a general statement that can be drawn from the information you have collected. Your conclusion needs to be supported by the evidence you have gathered.

Persuasive Essay Builders
What is my topic?
What is my stance (how I feel about the issue)?
Who is my audience?

What are the arguments against my stance?
How can I answer those arguments?

What are the arguments for my stance?
How can I support those arguments?

What is my conclusion about the topic?

WRITING LETTERS

Business Letters

Letters are types of non-fiction, too. A **business letter** is a letter written to a company or to the government. In it, you may request information, help, express your thanks, or ask questions. The six parts to a business letter are the heading, inside address, greeting or salutation, body, closing, and signature.

- The **heading** is the address of the person who is writing the letter. Write the date under the heading.
- The **inside address** is the name and address of the company to whom the letter is being written. Each important word of the company's name begins with a capital letter.
- The **greeting** or **salutation** is the way the writer says hello. Use a colon after the greeting.
- The **body** is what is written to the company.
- The **closing** is the way the writer says good-bye. The closing always begins with a capital letter and ends with a comma. For a business letter, always say *Thank You* or *Sincerely*.
- The **signature** is the name of the person who wrote the letter.

---

207 Hope Street   _ **Heading**
Alpine, OR 97408

June 10, 2003

Sirs Import and Export, Inc.   _ **Inside Address**
64 Seventh Street
New York, NY 10022

Dear Sir: _ **Greeting/Salutation**

I have not yet received the three cartons of heirloom seeds I ordered from your company three weeks ago. I would appreciate it if this problem could be taken care of as soon as possible. _ **Body**

             Closing _   Sincerely,

                 Allan Baynes

             Signature _   Allan Baynes

Friendly Letters

Write a **friendly letter** as a thank-you note to someone you know well, an invitation to a party, a pen pal letter, or a letter to someone your own age.

The five parts of a friendly letter are the **heading**, **greeting**, **body**, **closing**, and **signature**. The heading of the letter can be the date or the address to which you are sending the letter. Use the greeting *Dear,* and follow it with a comma instead of a colon. In the body, write the main content of the letter. For the closing, use the word with which you feel most comfortable: *Love, Your Friend, Sincerely, Best Wishes, With Love, Many Thanks, Thank you, or Warm Regards.* Finish the letter by signing your name.

Heading _ Feb. 16, 2003

Dear Miss Judy,   _ **Greeting**

Thank you so much for being my piano teacher. I feel like I have learned so much over the past year. I really appreciate all the time you spent helping me get ready for the school talent show.

I'm sorry that we are moving and I won't get to be your student anymore. I'll miss our Tuesday practices. I promise I will keep in touch and let you know about my new teacher.

Thanks again for all your help. I will miss you! _ **Body**

Closing _   Your Friend,

Signature _ *Casey*

Envelopes

Every envelope should have the following details: **return address**, **mailing address**, and **stamp**. In a business letter, the first line of the mailing address should have the name and title of the person you want to receive the letter. The second line should have the name of the company. The third line is the street address, and the fourth line is the city, state, and zip code. For a friendly letter, you will not need to write a company name.

Barry Studios   _ **Return Address**
212 Straight A Ranch Rd.
Intelligence, AZ 85726

Mailing Address _   Mr. Michael Messa, President
Think Tank, Inc.
1026 Aikew Blvd.
Jenius, Texas 76722

WRITING ASSESSMENT

Rubrics

A **rubric** is a list of things your writing must do in order to get a certain grade. Rubrics usually have levels that are graded by numbers (1, 2, 3, 4), or words (beginning, satisfactory, capable, excellent). Each level is a little different. The teacher reads the paper and decides which category the paper fits into.

Even if your teacher doesn't use rubrics in your class, you can use these examples to help you write a better paper. If your teacher says he or she is "looking for" something in your paper, write those things down on the blank rubric. If your teacher gives you a rubric, put it in your writing folder. Then when you're in the revising stage, read your rubric and then read your paper carefully. Decide if there is anything you can do to improve your paper.

In the sample below, there are notes and tips in the parenthesis to help you understand the elements. Read each list carefully, and then decide what level your paper has achieved based on the **Scoring Levels**. Write your scoring level next to the element. Then go back to your paper and make changes to improve your score. After you've made your changes, come back to the rubric and go through it again. Do this as many times as you need to until your paper is just the way you want it.

Sample Writing Rubric
Key Elements

__ Idea Development
The paper has a main topic and facts and details that support that main topic. The introduction introduces the main idea. Each paragraph helps to develop the idea. The conclusion uses a summary to restate the main ideas.

__ Organization
Each paragraph has a topic sentence and sentences that support the topic sentence. The paper is organized in chronological (time) order (like a history essay), by three to four main points (like an animal or sports report), or from least to most specific point (like a science report).

__ Language Usage
The writer uses language correctly, including homophones and commonly misused words (check out the guide in **Section 2: Usage**). The writer uses words correctly according to their parts of speech (for example no verbs are used as adjectives). The writer also avoids double negatives, uses pronouns properly, and makes subjects and verbs agree (check out tips in **Section 5: Style**).

__ Sentence Structure
The writer uses a variety of sentence types (simple, compound, compound-complex, and complex) and a variety of sentence lengths (count your words). There are no fragments or run-ons.

__ Mechanics
The writer uses correct spelling, capitalization, and punctuation. Every paragraph is indented.

Scoring Levels
0 points—no key elements evident
1 point—beginning...few key elements evident
2 points—satisfactory...all 5 key elements evident to a moderate degree
3 points—capable...all 5 key elements evident ranging from moderate to high degree
4 points—excellent...all 5 key elements evident consistently to a high degree

Your Personal Writing Rubric
Key Elements

__ 1. _____
   _____
   _____

__ 2. _____
   _____
   _____

__ 3. _____
   _____
   _____

__ 4. _____
   _____
   _____

__ 5. _____
   _____
   _____

Scoring levels
0 points—no key elements evident
1 point—beginning...few key elements evident
2 points—satisfactory...all 5 key elements evident to a moderate degree
3 points—capable...all 5 key elements evident ranging from moderate to high degree
4 points—excellent...all 5 key elements evident consistently to a high degree

Checklists

A **checklist** is like a rubric because both are lists of things you should do in your paper. A checklist, however, does not have a grade that goes with it. When you go through a checklist, make notes of what you need to do to improve your paper, and give yourself credit for what you are already doing well. The checklist is here to help you check yourself and your work before you hand it in. In the samples below, you'll find lists of things to help you focus on one part of your paper. Use these ideas during the revising process to help you improve your work without worrying too much about the grading.

Organization Checklist

__ Events and Ideas in Order that Makes Sense
Use chronological (time) order for history, specific points (see the "Life in France" example under **How to Write an Outline**), or least to most specific for a science paper.

__ Main Idea in Each Paragraph
Every paragraph has a topic sentence. Reread each topic sentence. Separate it into complete subject and predicate. Then separate the simple subject and predicate. Is the sentence direct? Does it say what you want it to say?

__ Details, Descriptions, Examples Focus on Topic
Every sentence in a paragraph relates back to the main idea. It gives a fact or detail to support the main idea. Go back to your outline. Does every sentence in your paragraph relate back to something you wrote in your outline?

__ Ending Summarizes Main Ideas/Points Made
The conclusion should be a summary of the main points of the essay. Don't introduce new facts or details. Don't list every detail again. Reread your topic sentences and make a list of the main points they make. Then restate these points in the conclusion.

Usage and Style Checklist (review **Section 2: Usage** and **Section 5: Style**)

__ Language Usage
The writer uses language correctly, including homophones and commonly misused words (check out the guide in **Section 2: Usage**). The writer uses words correctly according to their parts of speech (for example no verbs are used as adjectives) and makes subjects and verbs agree.

__ Uses Formal Language
The writer avoids contractions, slang, clichés, and idioms. The writer avoids sloppy speech (gonna, coulda, hafta). The writer also avoids double negatives and uses pronouns properly.

__ Sentence Structure
The writer uses a variety of sentence types (simple, compound, compound-complex, and complex) and a variety of sentence lengths (count your words). There are no fragments or run-ons.

__ Formatting
The writer indents each paragraph. The writer uses punctuation correctly. The writer has the title, his or her name, the date, and the page numbers written or typed on the paper.

SECTION 5
STYLE

Style is important to all writers. Style describes the quality of your writing: Are the sentences clear? Are the length and type of sentences varied throughout the paragraph? Do the sentences flow together smoothly? Do all the sentences in a paragraph stay on topic? This section on style is focused on helping you write the clearest, best quality sentences and paragraphs that you can. You'll find tips for improving your sentences and paragraphs and advice on how to make them flow and work together better. Every sentence will say what you want it to say, and every paragraph will stay on topic and flow smoothly.

RULES FOR BETTER SENTENCES

Remove Extra Words
Tighten wordy sentences by removing extra words. Read each sentence. Condense it into a simple subject and a simple predicate. Then consider the complete subject and complete predicate. Does your point come across without all the extra words?

     Slaves were portrayed or stereotyped as…

Take out the word *portrayed*. You don't need both *portrayed* and *stereotyped* to get your point across.

Parallel Construction
All parts of a sentence should be alike, or parallel. When writing lists, make sure that each part of the list is written in the same way. Pay special attention to gerunds and infinitives, and be careful when you write comparisons.

    Wrong: The horses were sleek, streamlined, and fed proper food.
    Right: The horses were sleek, streamlined, and properly fed.

    Wrong: The group likes to swim, to ski, and go fishing.
    Right: The group likes to swim, to ski, and to fish.

    Wrong: Going to the store is not as interesting as it is to watch a movie.
    Right: Going to the store is not as interesting as watching a movie.

    Wrong: To drive at night is more difficult than daylight driving.
    Right: Nighttime driving is more difficult than daylight driving.

Subjects That Follow Verbs
When subjects follow verbs, make sure that the subject and verb agree in number.

    At the back of the room are several empty chairs.

Several empty chairs is the subject of the sentence, so the verb, *are*, must agree with this plural subject. *At the back of the room* is a prepositional phrase, not the subject.

Add Needed Words
When you make sentences parallel, don't forget to add any words you may need around conjunctions.

Incorrect: Some clubs believe and live by the old rules.
You can't "believe by" something.
Correct: Some clubs believe in and live by the old rules.
You "believe in" and "live by."

Give More Detail

Nouns are sometimes used within a sentence in an **appositive**, a word or phrase set off by commas that identifies or gives further details about another noun. The examples below show how an appositive expands a sentence.

> **OK:** Abraham Lincoln gave his most famous speech at a dedication ceremony for a Civil War cemetery.
> **Better:** Abraham Lincoln gave his most famous speech, the Gettysburg Address, at a dedication ceremony for a Civil War cemetery.
> **OK:** Ms. Walker was out of breath from racing Craig.
> **Better:** Ms. Walker was out of breath from racing Craig, the fastest boy in our class.

Avoid Shifts in Verb Tense

When you start a sentence in the present tense, try to stay in the present tense.

> **Incorrect:** She patted the puppy's head to wake it. Finally it *opens* its eyes.
> **Correct:** She patted the puppy's head to wake it. Finally it *opened* its eyes.

Avoid Misplaced Words

Reread your sentences and make sure all adverbs are placed as close as possible to the words they modify.

> **Incorrect:** You will *only* need to plant *one* packet of seeds.
> **Correct:** You will need to plant *only one* packet of seeds.

Misplaced and Dangling Modifiers

The complete subject or complete predicate of a sentence usually contains words or phrases called **modifiers**. Modifiers add to the meaning of a sentence.

> The ancient tombs, *which stand powerfully on the hot sands of Egypt,* are an amazing and wonderful sight.

Modifiers that are not placed near the words or phrases that they modify are called **misplaced modifiers**.

> **Misplaced:** *Scared to death,* the black night enveloped the lost student.
> **Correct:** *Scared to death,* the lost student wandered the neighborhood.

If a modifying word, phrase, or clause does not modify a particular word, it is called a **dangling modifier**. Every modifier must have a word that it clearly modifies.

> *Warmed by the sun,* it felt good to be at the beach.
> (dangling modifier—"warmed by the sun" does not modify "it")
> *Warmed by the sun,* we relaxed on our beach towels.
> (correct—"warmed by the sun" modifies "we")

Plural and Singular Antecedents

When replacing a noun with a pronoun, be sure the noun and pronoun agree in number. With some collective nouns, such as *team, class,* and *group,* you need to use a singular pronoun.

Correct: I asked how I could get on the soccer team, and *the team members* told me to try out for a position.

Incorrect: I asked how I could get on the soccer team, and *they* told me to try out.

Confusing Ownership

Frequently we come across sentences that can be understood in two or more ways.

Bad: Paul went with Dad to get his hat.

Whose hat is it? Paul's or Dad's? Instead of the pronoun "his," the writer should use the noun again.

Better: Paul went with Dad to get Dad's hat.

Formal Writing, Formal Language

In a formal paper like a report, business letter, or essay, it is better to use formal English. This means you should avoid using contractions, slang, clichés, idioms, and one-word sentences or interjections. Here are some examples from a business letter to help you.

Contractions

Bad: This wasn't what I expected when I ordered your product.

Better: This was not what I expected when I ordered your product.

Slang

Bad: This product really stinks and I want my money back.

Better: This product did not do what it was supposed to do, and I would like a refund.

Clichés and Idioms

Bad: Don't get hung up on excuses, just send me my money.

Better: I would appreciate an immediate refund.

Interjections

Bad: Really! I can't believe your company is still in business.

Better: Thank you for your attention to this matter.

Sloppy Speech

Sloppy speech is another thing you should avoid in formal writing. When we speak with our friends or family, we often use sloppy speech—slurring two words into one. This is okay for speech, but be sure to use the full words in your formal writing. The only time you might want to use these slurred words is when writing dialogue to develop the speaker's character.

Common Sloppy Speech

woulda	would have
gotta	got to
wanna	want to

Avoid Double Negatives

Two negatives equal a positive. Therefore, if you want a sentence to have a negative meaning, use only one negative word.

Wrong: I hardly never do that!
Right: I hardly ever do that!

Wrong: I don't understand none of this.
Right: I don't understand any of this.

The exception to this rule is the correlative conjunction pair *neither/nor*.

Negative words

aren't	haven't	nothing
barely	isn't	nowhere
can't	neither	scarcely
couldn't	never	shouldn't
didn't	no	wasn't
doesn't	no one	weren't
don't	nobody	won't
hardly	none	wouldn't
hasn't	not	

Positive words

any, some	do	should
anybody, somebody	does	someone
anyone	either	sometimes
anything, something	ever	somewhere
anywhere	had	was
are	has	were
can	have	will
could	is	would
did	or	yes, any

RULES FOR BETTER PARAGRAPHS

Have Structure

Every paragraph should start with a main idea or topic sentence. The topic sentence should sum up all the information that will be discussed in the paragraph, or it should introduce a new topic. All sentences after the topic sentence should relate to the topic. Every sentence should support the topic sentence with a detail or fact. Try to have at least three sentences in a paragraph. It is better to have five to seven.

Try to stick to one main sequence style for all your paragraphs. Either list things in chronological order, from least specific to most specific, or by importance level.

Make Sentences Flow

Using transition words in sentences and paragraphs is another practice good writers employ. Transition words help the reader understand and move forward through the piece of writing.

Time words: *before, during, after, when, first, second, next, then, lastly, finally, soon, later, meanwhile*

Compare or contrast words: *like, likewise, similarly, in the same way, as well as, but, however, nevertheless, yet, still, although*

Concluding words: *therefore, finally, lastly, in summary*

Provide Variety

You can also improve the flow of your sentences by varying the types of sentences you write. Start with a simple sentence. Then use a complex, compound-complex, or compound sentence. Try introducing a sentence with a prepositional phrase. Reports that use only declarative sentences can get boring. Try using this variety, especially in your introduction and conclusion, to liven up your writing.

OK: Cheetahs run fast. They are the fastest animals on land. This report will tell all about the cheetah.

Better: On your mark, get set, go! They're off—every animal on Earth has entered this race to see who is the fastest. It looks like a close race. The ostrich, the kangaroo, and the jackrabbit have passed the human entry. But far in the lead are the pronghorn and the cheetah. The cheetah sprints by at 63 miles per hour to win the race. What makes a cheetah a cheetah? How is this speedy animal different from other cats? Read on to find out.

Vary Sentence Length

Varying your sentence lengths is another way to add variety to your writing. A story or article full of short sentences would be choppy and annoying. Likewise, a piece of writing with long and windy sentences would confuse a reader. Count the length of your own sentences during the revision phase of your writing.

Avoid Rambling

The paragraph below contains some good ideas, but the sentences are too long and rambling. As you read, think about how you would change it by removing words, adding words, or adding punctuation.

Michael Jordan is my favorite athlete and I think he is the greatest basketball player ever and maybe the greatest athlete of any sport and Michael Jordan played for the Chicago Bulls and when he was on their team, the Bulls won the NBA championship in 1991 and 1992 and 1993 and 1996 and 1997 and 1998. I think Michael is a strong, powerful player but the reason he is so good is because whenever he plays he gives his best he doesn't get lazy and not try he always tries hard and he's the greatest!

Avoid Split Infinitives

An **infinitive** is a present tense verb preceded by the word *to* (to + verb = infinitive). An infinitive can act as a noun, an adjective, or an adverb.

George sat on the front step *to finish* his ice-cream cone.

Avoid splitting infinitives, or separating to and the verb.

Incorrect: This was his only chance *to* really *run* the race as hard as he could.

Correct: This was his only chance *to run* the race as hard as he could.

Hyperbole: Knowing When to Exaggerate

The literary term for exaggeration is **hyperbole**. When you say you are starving to death, even though you ate a sandwich an hour ago, you are using hyperbole. Hyperbole works well in stories. It adds depth to characters, and it can make a situation funny, scary, or tense. Hyperbole does not work so well in formal writing. For reports, essays, and business letters, you should stick to the facts. Saying that something is the best or worst of all time does not really tell your reader anything. Here are some examples.

OK: When Abraham Lincoln was assassinated, it was the worst day in American history.

Better: The nation mourned the loss of its president with a heavy heart.

OK: Everyone should wear X-Brand sneakers.

Better: If you are a volleyball or broomball player, I recommend X-Brand sneakers.

SUPER SENTENCE CHECKLIST

Use this checklist to think about the sentences you've written for stories, reports, essays, or other writing projects.

Basics

Yes   No

☐   ☐   Do your sentences begin with capital letters?

☐   ☐   Do your sentences end with the correct punctuation marks?

☐   ☐   Does each sentence have a subject and a verb?

Beyond Basics

Yes   No

☐   ☐   Do your sentences vary in length—short, medium, long?

☐   ☐   Do you use a variety of sentence types?

☐   ☐   Do you use creative words to help your reader picture what is being described?

☐   ☐   Do you begin your sentences in different ways?

☐   ☐   Do you use transition words to make the sentences flow?
(First, next, then, meanwhile, on the other hand, however, yet, still, in addition to, finally, lastly, in summary)

SECTION 6
RESEARCH

Being able to research a topic is a skill that you can use, not only in future classes at school, but also as you become interested in topics in your everyday life.

Research is nothing to fear. When you have a topic in mind and are ready to find information on it at the library, think of your research as a treasure hunt. You will look in many different places to find all of the information you need. Along the way, you will discover many valuable books, magazines, reference tools, and other materials that you probably never knew existed.

When you write a research-based paper, you have to make sure that your information has order, clarity, and can be understood by someone who has not done all of the research you have. If you take the time to carefully gather your information, organize it, and then write your paper, you should have a great report that others will enjoy reading.

Although writing a report requires a lot of hard work sometimes, remember that you are learning all by yourself, outside of the classroom. You can be proud that when you finish your research, your report reflects information that you gathered and organized on your own. You have taught yourself, and you should feel proud of the work you've done.

In this section, you'll find an important part on avoiding plagiarism. You'll also find information on the library and how to use the reference books—encyclopedias, dictionaries, atlases—you will find there. Also included is information on caring for books, the Dewey Decimal System, and the different parts of a book. With the tips you will learn here, you can research any topic.

AVOIDING PLAGIARISM

What Is Plagiarism?
Plagiarism is a current, serious issue for students, teachers, and schools throughout the country. *To plagiarize* means to copy someone else's ideas and submit them as your own, without giving that person credit. This is wrong for many reasons. When you pass off someone else's ideas as your own, you are being dishonest. Plagiarism is a form of stealing. You must always give credit to the authors and books that you used to find details, facts, or ideas for any of your writing. This is why you write a bibliography.

Plagiarism can have serious consequences, so it is important to get into the habit of avoiding it early on. In high school, you may fail a class if you are caught plagiarizing. Colleges and universities throw out students who plagiarize. When people copy in the work place, they are often fired and may even face criminal charges.

It's not just the consequences that make plagiarism bad. When you plagiarize, you are cheating yourself. Who knows how well you could have written the report if you had just tried? When you copy, you don't give yourself the chance to succeed.

How Can I Avoid Plagiarism?

The best thing to do to avoid plagiarism is to be conscious of it. If you make an effort when you research, you can easily avoiding copying.

- Always close a book before you write down a fact from it. Restate the fact in your own words.
- When you write down a quote, put it in quotation marks in your notes so you will remember that it is a quote. Write down the page number the quote is on, too.
- When you write down facts, dates, and other statistics, write down only the numbers. Do not write the whole sentence in which the fact appears. This will help you to write the information in your own words later.
- Never copy anything word for word without quotation marks around it.
- Remember that you must cite Internet sources just as you would cite a book or magazine.

THE LIBRARY

Fiction

Fiction is made up. It may be based on truth, but it is not one hundred percent true. There are many different types of fiction. These types are called *genres*. A few fiction *genres* are science fiction, mystery, historical fiction, realistic fiction, and western fiction. Many libraries have separate sections for these genres. They may also have a special sticker on the spine of a book to identify its genre. Fiction is filed in alphabetical order.

Non-Fiction

Non-Fiction books are completely true. There are many different genres of non-fiction, too. Some of them include biography, autobiography, how-to books, fact books, and poetry. The non-fiction section of a library is separated from the fiction, and it is filed using the Dewey Decimal System.

Indexes and Bibliography

In the Dewey Decimal Bibliography, you can find different types of indexes that will help you find articles in magazines or journals about the topic of your choice. Be sure to check the magazine guide to see which magazines are indexed. The library may not have copies of all the magazines used in the index.

Reference

The Reference section of the library has books that cannot be checked out. They are there all the time for everyone to use. You will find dictionaries, thesauruses, encyclopedias, almanacs, atlases, and other types of informative books in the reference section. You may need to ask a librarian for permission to use materials from this section.

Other Library Sections

Libraries usually have children's sections where fiction and non-fiction books for children are separated from those meant for adults. Libraries also have audio-visual materials, such as CDs, tapes, DVDs, and videocassettes. Music is filed in alphabetical order by genre (jazz, rock, pop, classical, etc.). Non-fiction movies are filed in the Dewey Decimal System, and fiction movies are in alphabetical order.

Libraries also have periodicals. Periodicals are materials such as newspapers, magazines, and journals that are printed over certain periods of time. Magazines and newspapers are valuable resources because they have current information that may not be available in books yet.

Library Alphabetical Order

When putting books in alphabetical order, look at the first letters of the first word after *a*, *an*, or *the*. The book *The Great Gatsby* will be shelved in *G* under *Great*, not *T* under *The*. If the first words are the same, look at the second words: *The Great Gatsby* will be after *The Great Escape*.

The Dewey Decimal System

Mevil Dewey, from Adams Center, New York, created the Dewey Decimal Classification

System for small libraries in 1876. It separates non-fiction books into 100 different divisions, so that books with similar topics are numbered and filed together. During his life, Dewey helped to start the American Library Association. He also created Columbia University's School of Library Economy, which was the start of library science in the United States.

*The Dewey Decimal System
000-099 General Reference (dictionary, encyclopedia)
100-199 Philosophy and Psychology (ideas of humankind)
200-299 Religion
300-399 Social Science (fairy tales, fables, government, laws)
400-499 Language
500-599 Science (rocks, animals, insects)
600-699 Useful Arts (cooking, pet care, farming)
700-799 Fine Arts (sports, arts and crafts, photography)
800-899 Literature (poems, plays, short stories)
900-999 Geography and History (atlas, travel, biography, history)
*You can see the 100 Divisions in Appendix 4 at the back of this book.

Sometimes you will visit the library and ask: Where do I begin to look? What section of the Dewey Decimal System will help me? Think about what you are looking for. Ask yourself three questions:

What do I really need?
Where can I find it?
How much information do I need?

Here is an example. Mike needs information about space travel and satellites. What does he need? He needs information about space satellites. Where can he find it? Look at the Dewey chart. The 600-699 section (useful arts) has books about transportation including space. Now how much information does he need? He needs enough information for a report. At least two or three books will help.

It is also a good idea to clearly define your research topic. If you are clear about the subject, it will be easier to choose a Dewey section.

Understanding the "Decimal" in the Dewey Decimal System
In using the library, you have probably noticed that the class numbers of some books contain *decimals* (a period called a "decimal point" followed by one or more numbers). Each book falls into one of the 100 divisions. Within each division there are further divisions. For example, 790 is "Recreation and Performing Arts." Within 790, there are 9 different divisions, 791 through 799. 796 is "athletic and outdoor sports and games." Under 796, there are unlimited divisions, depending on the decimal added to the end of the number. For example, 796.1 is "miscellaneous games." 796.357 is "baseball."

Remember from math class that 796.3 is less than 796.31, so 796.3 will come before 796.31 on the shelf. Under each call number is a letter. This letter is the first letter of the author's last name. This letter is used to put books in both decimal and alphabetical order. In 796.357, there may be 30 books about baseball. The first letter of each author's last name

is used to put these books in order. A book by Adamson will come before Adler.

Using the Catalog—Choosing an Entry

You need information quickly, and you want to find it easily. How do you find what you want? Use the catalog. Today most library catalogs are computerized, but some libraries still have card catalogs. The library catalog is divided into three to five sections: author, title, and subject are the most common searches. You may also have the option to search for a book using keywords or the call number. The information is the same for every catalog entry. You will find the call number telling the location of the book (children's fiction, young adult fiction, adult mystery). The entry will also have the book title, author, place of publication, publisher, copyright date, and a brief summary of the contents or topic of the book.

Before you begin a search, ask yourself: Do you have the author's name? Do you have the title of the book? Do you have the subject? Here's an example. Your teacher assigned a report about the weather. Do you have the author's name? No. Do you have the title of the book? No. Do you have the subject? Yes. You can look under weather as a subject or as a keyword.

BOOKS

Caring for Books

You may have heard this a million times before, but it is important to care for your books, especially ones you borrow from the library. Libraries don't have a lot of money to spend on repairing books, and some libraries may give you a fine if you return books badly damaged. It is so easy to care for books!

- Always make sure your hands are clean when you handle a book.
- Turn pages carefully.
- Never write in a book.
- Keep food, drinks, and pets away from books.
- Only mark your place in the book with a bookmark.

Parts of a Book

Knowing the parts of a book make it easier to find the information you need. Look at the **spine** of the book to find the title, author, call numbers, and the publisher's name. The call numbers tell you where to find the book in the library.

The **title page** tells you the author, title, and publisher's name. On the back of the title page is the **copyright page**. This page will tell you where the book was printed and in what year. You will need this information for your bibliography.

The **table of contents** tells you the name of each chapter. It may even have an outline of the chapter, telling you where to find the beginning of each new topic.

At the back of the book, you may find a **glossary** and an **index**. A glossary gives the definitions of words used in the book that you may not know. The index lists topics in alphabetical order. Next to the topic is the page number(s) where you can find information about the topic in the book. This is very helpful if you are looking for a date, someone's name, or a specific fact. The index is much more specific than the table of contents.

Another reference you may find at the end of a book is an **appendix**. An appendix gives more information about a specific topic that either relates to the content of the book or was briefly mentioned in the book. For example, in a biography about an author's life, one appendix may list all the books the author wrote in chronological order. Another appendix might have the author's family tree. A final appendix may have a list of important events in history that happened during the author's life.

A **bibliography** lists the titles, authors, and publishing information of other books about the same topic or that the author used while writing his or her own book.

Visual Aids

Charts, graphs, tables, time lines, and other visual aids can be found in many books. If you take the time to study them, these visual aids will show you how information, facts and ideas relate to one another. They also show you how to draw conclusions from what you have learned in your reading.

In order to understand a visual aid, you have to be able to read one correctly. First read all the text surrounding the visual aid. Then follow these steps.

- Read the title to find out what the visual aid is about.
- Read each label to know what each section or part means.
- Start at the top and work through the visual aid to get the details or specific parts of information.
- Draw conclusions from the information.

REFERENCE BOOKS

Encyclopedias

Comparing Encyclopedia Indexes

Each encyclopedia has one volume that lists the articles in the encyclopedia alphabetically. This volume is called an index. Use the index to quickly find the information you need. You will not find the same information in every encyclopedia, so compare encyclopedia indexes when you are collecting your research.

Encyclopedia of Plants		*Plant Encyclopedia*	
Gardening	flowers F- 501	Gardening	flowers, types F- 376
	plants P-665		flowers, when to cut F-379
	seeds, types S- 315		gardening tools G- 317
	seeds, potting S-311		how to buy seeds S-271

As you can see, the first entry from the *Encyclopedia of Plants* has different information than the second entry from *Plant Encyclopedia*. Depending upon the topic of your paper, the information in *Plant Encyclopedia* may be more useful than the information in *Encyclopedia of Plants*.

Use With Caution

After using the encyclopedia index, look up the entry. The encyclopedia is often the first place you should look for information. It gives you a broad overview of the topic with lots of facts. It will not always give you interesting details that can give your report color and life though.

If you use only the encyclopedia to write your report, your teacher will be able to tell, and your report will not be very interesting. You should also keep in mind that the more specific your topic is, the less likely the encyclopedia will have information on it. For example, the encyclopedia has a lot of information on dogs, but if your report is about a specific breed of dog, such as greyhounds, you will find less information on the specific breed in the encyclopedia.

Dictionaries

Why Use a Dictionary?

When Mr. Webster first wrote the dictionary, he did it so that our writing and spelling would be more standardized. This standardization is still important today, but there are many other reasons to use the dictionary.

- We learn how to spell words.
- We learn how to pronounce words.
- We learn what words mean.
- We learn what parts of speech words are.
- We learn the origin of words.

Types of Dictionaries

There are many types of dictionaries, so it is important to decide what type you need before you start your search for an unknown word. Children who do not read can use a picture dictionary. It has pictures to give the meanings of words.

If you are researching a person for your report, you can use the biographical dictionary to look up basic facts about the person, much like how you would use the encyclopedia for an overview. By reading the entry on the person you are researching, you will likely get more ideas about what you want to write about in your report and what resources you can look up next.

A foreign language dictionary has two parts: one side that is in English and the other that is in a specific foreign language. When you look up a word in English, it tells you the word in the other language. When you look up a word in the foreign language, it tells you the word in English.

Doctors and nurses use medical dictionaries to help them with the words they use everyday. Many other professions have specialized dictionaries as well. You will most likely want a standard English dictionary, which contains words, their meanings, their parts of speech, their pronunciations, and their origins, all in English.

How to Use the Dictionary

Study the dictionary entries below. Notice how much you can learn about a word from the dictionary.

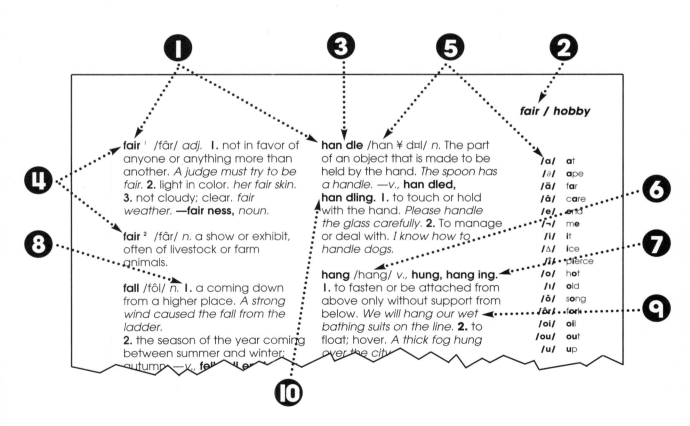

fair / hobby

fair /fâr/ *adj.* **1.** not in favor of anyone or anything more than another. *A judge must try to be fair.* **2.** light in color. *her fair skin.* **3.** not cloudy; clear. *fair weather.* **—fair ness,** *noun.*

fair ² /fâr/ *n.* a show or exhibit, often of livestock or farm animals.

fall /fôl/ *n.* **1.** a coming down from a higher place. *A strong wind caused the fall from the ladder.* **2.** the season of the year coming between summer and winter; autumn —v., **fell, fall en.**

han dle /han ¥ dəl/ *n.* The part of an object that is made to be held by the hand. *The spoon has a handle.* —v., **han dled, han dling. 1.** to touch or hold with the hand. *Please handle the glass carefully.* **2.** To manage or deal with. *I know how to handle dogs.*

hang /hang/ *v.*, **hung, hang ing. 1.** to fasten or be attached from above only without support from below. *We will hang our wet bathing suits on the line.* **2.** to float; hover. *A thick fog hung over the city.*

/a/	at
/ə/	ape
/ä/	far
/â/	care
/e/	end
/ē/	me
/i/	it
/ī/	ice
/î/	pierce
/o/	hot
/ī/	old
/ô/	song
/âr/	fork
/oi/	oil
/ou/	out
/u/	up

1. The **entry word** is the word you look up. Entry words are in bold type and listed in alphabetical order.

2. At the top of each dictionary page are two words called **guide words**. They are the first and last entry words appearing on that page. Guide words help you find an entry word quickly.

3. Words with more than one syllable are shown in two parts. A space separates the syllables.

4. Sometimes there is more than one entry word. When this happens, each entry is numbered.

5. After the entry word is the pronunciation. It is given between two lines. Special letters are used to show how to pronounce the word. A pronunciation key shows the sound for each special letter. The pronunciation key is found at the beginning, end, or on each page of the dictionary.

6. An abbreviation for the part of speech of the entry word is given after the pronunciation.

7. The dictionary also shows irregular forms of the entry word. If an *s, es, ed,* or *ing* is simply added to the word, the dictionary does not list these regularly spelled forms.

8. One or more definitions are given for each entry word. If more than one definition is listed, the definitions are numbered.

9. Sometimes the entry word is used in a sample sentence or phrase to help explain the meaning of the word.

10. Some words can be more than one part of speech. If so, the dictionary sometimes gives another definition for the entry word.

Multiple Meaning Words

Many words have more than one meaning. The word *set* has the largest number of definitions, with some dictionaries listing almost 200 different meanings. If the definitions of a word are closely related, they usually are listed under the same entry word. However, if a word has meanings that are unrelated, they usually are listed separately.

de·sert (dĕz rt) **n.** 1. dry land receiving little rainfall. 2. empty, uncultivated area; wasteland.—**adj.** 3. having to do with dry land or its vegetation. 4. sparsely occupied or unoccupied; desert island.

de·sert (dĭzėrt') **v.** 1. abandon, withdraw. 2. to leave the military without permission.—**n.** deserter

de·sert (dĭzėrt') **n.** deserved reward or punishment, usually plural. *He received his just deserts.*

Almanacs

When is Herbert Hoover's birthday? Who is the governor of Tennessee? How many breeds of dog are there? All these questions can be answered by the almanac. An almanac is a reference book full of odd and unusual facts that is published once a year. However, it also contains statistics and facts from previous years. If you need specific information that is more recent than what can be found in books or encyclopedias, the almanac can help you. Interesting and commonly unknown facts can liven up a research report if the information is presented appropriately.

Since an almanac is not organized in alphabetical order, you need to know the key word of the information you're looking for so that you can use the index to look up the fact you need. In an almanac, the index is located at the front of the book. There, the key words or subject headings are listed alphabetically. The main subject headings are in bold face type. The subheadings relating to the main headings are indented under the main headings.

You can find information on the following topics and many, many more in an almanac:

actors	history
artists	other countries
astronauts	pets
athletes	presidents
constellations	solar system
country flags	sports
each state	top television programs
exports and imports	weather
geography	

Atlases

If you are researching a location for your report, such as a continent, foreign country or city, or even a body of water, the atlas is definitely a resource you should look into. The maps in an atlas go way beyond cities and boundaries. Maps can show populations, climates, crops, weather systems, resources and products, and any physical information, including the height of mountains. Atlases are especially fun to use because there is very little reading involved—all of the information is in picture form.

There are three main types of maps. A **relief map** shows the physical geography of a country. A **political map** shows nations, countries, state boundaries, and important cities. An **economic map** shows where products are grown or made, including cattle, wheat, and steel. There are other types of maps. These show climate, population, transportation, precipitation (rain and snowfall), and time zones. Use the index to locate the type of map you want. Once you've found a useful map, you'll need to know how to read it.

Legend or Key
The legend or key will help you read a map. It tells you what the different colors, symbols, and other markings on a map mean. It also tells you the scale, or size, of the map compared to real distance.

Symbols

Symbols on an atlas stand for a condition or feature of the landscape. They can represent human-made things like roads, railroad tracks, or airports, as well as natural features, like mountains, lakes, and rivers. Look to the legend or key to tell you what each symbol means.

Thesaurus

The thesaurus is a useful tool for expanding vocabulary, which adds variety to speech and writing. A thesaurus is a list of words and their synonyms. You will also find a few antonyms for each word.

A thesaurus is arranged alphabetically. Each entry contains the entry word and a list of synonyms. The antonyms are at the end of the definition. There are guide words at the top of each page, just like a dictionary. Not every word is in the thesaurus. Most words in the thesaurus are adjectives, nouns, or verbs.

Use the thesaurus's synonyms to replace overused, unclear, and weak words. You should also replace words that are not descriptive.

Use the antonym entries to write strong contrasts. To contrast one item from another, use antonyms from a thesaurus to describe the two things as differently as possible.

SECTION 7
SPELLING

Use the vowel chart, consonant chart, and 12 spelling rules on the following pages to help you check your work and improve your spelling.

VOWEL SOUNDS

Sound	Sign	Spelling	Spelling Tip
short a	/a/	lamp	The short a sound is often spelled *a*.
short o	/o/	crop	The short o sound is often spelled *o*.
short e	/e/	fence ready	The short e sound is often spelled *e* and *ea*.
short i	/i/	risk	The short i sound is often spelled *i*.
short u	/u/	dusk	The short u sound is often spelled *u*.
long a	/ā/	flame	The long a sound is spelled *a_e*, *ai*, and *ay*.
long o	/ō/	spoke	The long o sound is spelled *o_e* and *oa*.
long e	/ē/	clean keep	The long e sound is often spelled *ea* and *ee*.
long i	/ī/	wise high guide giant	The long i sound is often spelled *i_e* and *igh*. It can also be spelled *ie*, *ia*, *ei*, *uy*, and *ui*.
/aw/	/aw/	awful fault	The /aw/ sound is often spelled *aw* and *au*.
/ü/	/ü/	flute root grew	The /ü/ sound may be spelled *u_e*, *oo*, and *ew*. It can also be spelled *ou*, *ui*, and *o_e*.
/oi/	/oi/	join enjoy	The /oi/ sound may be spelled *oi* and *oy*
/ou/	/ou/	frown mouth	The /ou/ sound is often spelled *ow* and *ou*.
/ô/	/ô/	law pause moth	The /ô/ sound may be spelled *aw*, *au*, and *o*.
/âr/	/âr/	chair bear fare	The /âr/ sound can be spelled *air*, *ear*, and *are*.
/ûr/	/ûr/	burn	The /ûr/ sound is spelled *ur*.
/ôr/	/ôr/	storm tore	The /ôr/ sound is often spelled *or* and *ore*.
/əl/	/əl/	people pedal travel	The /əl/ sound, an unstressed syllable with the consonant l, may be spelled *le*, *el*, and *al*.

/ər/	/ər/	dollar	The /ər/ sound, an unstressed syllable with the consonant r, may be spelled *ar, er,* or *re.*
/it/	/it/	light	The /it/ sound is spelled *ight.*
/y/	/i/ or /ī/	cycle lyric	The /i/ and /ī/ sounds can both be spelled *y.*

CONSONANT SOUNDS

Sound	Spelling	Spelling Tip
/f/	foot enough	The /f/ sound can be spelled *f* or *gh* at the end of a word.
/h/	horse who	The /h/ sound may be spelled *h* and *wh.*
/j/	giant large	The /j/ sound is often spelled *g* and *ge.*
/k/	cake kilt lock	The /k/ sound can be spelled with a *c, k,* or *ck.*
/kw/	quit	The /kw/ sound is spelled *qu.*
/ks/	fix	The /ks/ sound is spelled *x.*
/n/	not knot	The /n/ sound can be spelled with a silent *k.*
/ng/	skunk hungry	The /ng/ sound can be spelled *n* or *ng.*
/r/	right write	The /r/ sound can be spelled with a silent *w.*
/s/	sink face	The /s/ sound is often spelled *s* and *c.*
/skw/	square	The /skw/ sound is spelled *squ.*
/wh/	white	The /wh/ sound is spelled *wh.*
/z/	rose zip	The /z/ sound may be spelled *s* or *z.*
middle consonant	letter	The middle consonant sound in some words may be spelled with double consonants.

12 SPELLING RULES

English spelling is crazy for the most part. However, there are a several patterns you can rely on to help you spell words correctly. On the following pages, you'll find a dozen spelling rules that are helpful. One hint in reading the rules: Take your time. Read each rule and example carefully and then stop to think about it. Try to relate the rules to the examples. Think of your own examples, too.

C-Enders

When *c* is the last letter of a word, it is always hard. That means it is pronounced like a *k*. When adding *ing, er,* or *y* to such words, first insert a *k*:

      panic—panicky
      picnic—picnicking
      traffic—trafficking

The *k* is said to "protect" the hard sound of the *c*. Without the *k*, the *c* might appear to have a soft sound (*s*) as it does in a word like *icing*.

Note that you don't add the *k* when the suffix begins with a consonant. When adding *ing* to *mimic*, for example, it becomes *mimicking*. But when the suffix *ry* is added, *mimic* becomes *mimicry* (the *k* is not needed to protect the *c* in this case).

Compound Words

When spelling a compound word—a word formed from two other words—keep both words whole. Do not drop the last letter of the first word. Do not drop the first letter of the last word. Simply push the two words together.

      side + walk = sidewalk

This rule is true even when the resulting compound words have a strange-looking double letter in the middle.

      book + keeper = bookkeeper
      hitch + hiker = hitchhiker
      room + mate = roommate

The classic exception to this rule is *pastime*.

      past + time = pastime

Contractions

Since many contractions have homonyms, mix-ups are common. Be sure you have the right word. The trick is to expand the contraction to be certain that you have the right word. Suppose you wrote:

      I gave the dog it's bone.

Try expanding *it's*. You get:

      I gave the dog it is bone.

The *it is* obviously makes no sense here. Thus, the correct word is *its*.

Remember to put the apostrophe in the right place. The apostrophe goes in the spot

where the letters were removed. Again, expanding the contraction is a good test. Suppose you wrote *are'nt*. Check it by expansion: *are'nt = are not*. The *o* in *not* is dropped in making this contraction. That means the apostrophe should go between the *n* and the *t*. Hence, the correct spelling is *aren't*.

Double-Enders
When the last two letters of a single-syllable word are a vowel followed by a consonant, double the consonant before adding a suffix.

> rip—ripper, ripping
> swim—swimmer, swimming
> top—topping, topped

The same rule holds for multiple-syllable words when the final syllable is accented.

> acquit—acquittal
> control—controlling
> submit—submitting

Note that words like *seat* become *seating* (one *t*) because there are two vowels before the final consonant. Words like *help* become *helping* (one *p*) because they end in two consonants. And words like *benefit* become *benefited* (one *t*) because they are not accented on the final syllable.

E-Enders
Many words end in a silent *e*. Two rules govern what happens to this *e* when you add suffixes.

First rule: Drop the *e* when the suffix begins with a vowel—*ed, ing, ous, able, y*.

> lose—losing
> louse—lousy
> nerve—nervous
> prove—provable
> tease—teasing

Important exceptions to this rule are *noticeable* and *courageous*. Also, with many words that end in *ve*, it is permissible to either drop or keep the *e* before *able*.

> love—lovable, loveable
> move—movable, moveable

Second rule: Keep the silent *e* when the suffix begins with a consonant—*ment, ful, ly*.

> care—careful
> move—movement

Judgment and *acknowledgment* (no *e*) were once exceptions to this rule, but now *judgement* and *acknowledgement* (with the *e*) are accepted. Two more exceptions—*truly* and *ninth*—drop the expected *e*'s.

Ful-Enders
Here's a truth that's short and sweet and very *powerful*. Words that end in *ful* and mean "full of" always end with *ful* (one *l*): *helpful, insightful, sorrowful*. There are no exceptions. Isn't that *wonderful*?

I Before E
The most famous spelling rule of all is a jingle that goes like this: *I before e except after c or when sounded as a as in neighbor or weigh.*

i before e	thief	yield
lie	field	

except after c	receive	receipt
conceive	deceive	

sounded as a	rein	heinous
reindeer	inveigh	

There is a problem with this classic truth. There are at least ten exceptions that "disprove" this rule. To remember them, think of this silly phrase: *Neither leisured foreign counterfeiter could seize either weird height without forfeiting protein.*

Ly-Enders
When the suffix *ly* is added to a word, that root word usually stays the same. Hence:
> clear—clearly
> sincere—sincerely
> slow—slowly
> undoubted—undoubtedly

Two well-known exceptions are *truly* (from *true*) and *wholly* (from *whole*).

This partial *ly* truth is especially helpful when facing words that end in *lly*.
> conceptual—conceptually
> hopeful—hopefully

When you're not sure if a word ends in *lly*, try to find the root. For example, *practically* comes from *practical*. The *ly* is simply tacked on to the end.

Nay-Sayers
Nearly a dozen prefixes turn root words into their opposites.
able—unable
possible—impossible
adjusted—maladjusted
sense—nonsense

The root never changes when a negative prefix is added. In *misshape* and *unnatural*, the double letters up front may look strange, but the rule holds firm. All you have to know for sure is how the root word begins.

Suppose, for example, you have written *unecessary* (one *n*). Is that correct? You know the word means "not necessary." *Necessary* is the root. To turn it into its antonym, you must add the prefix *un*. Hence *unnecessary* (two *n*'s) is the right spelling. The same goes for *illegal, misspell,* and *immature.*

Occasionally, you'll have a bit of trouble figuring out the root. *Innocent,* for example, is

based on *in-nocent* (*nocent* being Latin for "harmed"). Usually, though, the roots will be obvious, and you'll know to add the prefix.

> il**legible**
> ir**religious**

The Nay-Sayers' truth should also help you with words like *imagination* (one *m*). This is not a negative form because *agination* is not a word.

Ness-Enders
When adding the suffix *ness* to a root word, simply add the suffix. The root does not change unless it ends in *y* (happy—happiness).

> close—closeness
> helpful—helpfulness

Remembering that the root does not change will help you with tough words like:

> mean—meanness
> sudden—suddenness

O-Enders
Rules about plurals seems to multiply. Luckily, plurals don't cause many problems. Nouns that end in *o*, however, are tricky. The following observations may help.

If a vowel comes before the final *o*, add *s*:

> radio—radios
> rodeo—rodeos

If a consonant comes before the final *o*, add *es*:

> hero—heroes
> potato—potatoes

However, the plural forms of *mosquito* and *tornado* can go either way—*s* or *es*.

There is one general exception. The plural of most music-related, *o*-ending words are formed by adding *s* only.

> piano—pianos
> solo—solos

Y-Enders
When a word ends in *y*, change the *y* to *i* before adding the suffixes *ly, ness,* or *age*. You can slay some of the worst demons using this rule.

> busy—business
> day—daily
> easy—easily
> empty—emptiness
> lonely—loneliness
> penny—penniless
> marry—marriage
> satisfactory—satisfactorily
> temporary—temporarily

There are only a few exceptions.

shy—shyly
sly—slyly

Remember to keep the *y* when adding *ing* even though it may look a little odd.

HOW TO STUDY SPELLING WORDS

1. Look at the word.
2. Copy the word.
3. Say the word aloud.
4. Spell the word aloud.
5. Write the word.
6. Check the spelling.

You can also copy the following chart to help you study.

Copy the word.	Say it aloud. ✓	Spell it aloud. ✓	Close eyes. Spell it. ✓	Fold the paper. Write the word.
1.				1.
2.				2.
3.				3.
4.				4.
5.				5.
6.				6.
7.				7.
8.				8.
9.				9.
10.				10.
11.				11.
12.				12.
13.				13.
14.				14.
15.				15.
16.				16.
17.				17.
18.				18.
19.				19.
20.				20.

100 LIFELONG WORDS

Remember how to spell these frequently used and often misspelled words.

about	grade	something
address	guess	store
again		suppose
a lot	haven't	surprise
although	having	
always	hear	taught
around	heard	teacher
	here	their
because	hour	there
been	house	they're
before		thought
birthday	knew	threw
bought	know	through
busy		to
	language	together
calendar		tomorrow
children	many	tonight
come		too
coming	name	two
could	new	
couldn't	none	until
		used
didn't	often	
different	once	very
does	only	
doesn't	our	way
done		wear
	people	weight
early	picture	we're
easy	pretty	were
enough	probably	when
every		where
everybody	receive	which
	remember	while
favorite	right	women
first		would
friend	said	write
	school	
girl	should	your
goes	some	you're

MORE FREQUENTLY MISSPELLED WORDS

accept
absence
advice
all right
arctic
beginning
believe
bicycle
broccoli
bureau
ceiling
cemetery
changeable
conscious
decease
deceive
definite
descent
device
disastrous
embarrass
exercise
fascinate
February
fiery

fluorescent
foreign
government
grateful
guarantee
harass
height
humorous
independent
jealous
jewelry
judgment
ketchup
knowledge
leisure
library
license
maintenance
mathematics
miniature
miscellaneous
misspell
mysterious
necessary
neighbor

nuclear
occasion
occurrence
piece
pigeon
playwright
prejudice
privilege
probably
pumpkin
raspberry
rhythm
science
scissors
separate
sincerely
special
thorough
truly
Tuesday
until
Wednesday
weird

NATIONAL SPELLING BEE

The Louisville, Kentucky, *Courier-Journal* started the National Spelling Bee in 1925. They hoped that the cash prizes and the trip to the capital city would encourage spellers across the country to get involved.

In 1941, The Scripps Howard News Service took over the bee. There have been as few as 9 and as many as 250 contestants over the years. In 2002, Pratyush Buddiga, the 13-year-old champion, won $12,000 cash and other prizes for spelling *prospicience* correctly. Listed below are the winning words and some of their definitions.

2002 prospicience: the act of looking forward; foresight
2001 succedaneum: a person or thing that takes the place or function of another
2000 demarche: a course of action or maneuver
1999 logorrhea: excessive talkativeness or wordiness
1998 chiaroscurist: an artist who specializes in *chiaroscurro*
1997 euonym: a name well suited to the person, place, or thing named
1996 vivisepulture: the act or practice of burying alive
1995 xanthosis: yellow discoloration of the skin from abnormal causes
1994 antediluvian: made or developed a long time ago
1993 kamikaze: a member of the Japanese air attack corps assigned to make a suicida
     crash on a target
1992 lyceum: a hall for public lectures or discussions
1991 antipyretic: an agent that reduces fevers

1990 fibranne	1970 croissant	1950 haruspex	1930 fracas
1989 spoliator	1969 interlocutory	1949 dulcimer	1929 asceticism
1988 elegiacal	1968 abalone	1948 psychiatry	1928 albumen
1987 staphylococci	1967 chihuahua	1947 chlorophyll	1927 luxuriance
1986 odontalgia	1966 ratoon	1946 semaphore	1926 abrogate
1985 milieu	1965 eczema	1943-45 No Bee	1925 gladiolus
1984 luge	1964 sycophant	was held.	
1983 Purim	1963 equipage	1942 sacrilegious	
1982 psoriasis	1962 equamulose	1941 initials	
1981 sarcophagus	1961 smaragdine		
		1940 therapy	
1980 elucubrate	1960 troche	1939 canonical	
1979 maculature	1959 cacolet	1938 sanitarium	
1978 deification	1958 syllepsis	1937 promiscuous	
1977 cambist	1957 schappe	1936 intersning	
1976 narcolepsy	1956 condominium	1935 intelligible	
1975 incisor	1955 custaceology	1934 deteriorating	
1974 hydrophyte	1954 transept	1933 propitiatory	
1973 vouchsafe	1953 soubrette	1932 knack	
1972 macerate	1952 vignette	1931 foulard	
1971 shalloon	1951 insouciant		

SECTION 8
VOCABULARY

This vocabulary section is designed to help you read and write better. In the reader's vocabulary, you'll find tips on homonyms, root and base words, prefixes, and suffixes. Knowing about these types of words will help you build your vocabulary. The writer's vocabulary has information on figurative language and many ideas that you can use to improve your fiction writing.

Just remember that to correctly use vocabulary, you must understand the parts of speech and how they are used. For example, the word *excruciating* is an excellent adjective to describe great pain. "My toothache was *excruciating*." However, if you use the word as a verb, "My toothache *excruciating* me," or as a noun, "The *excruciating* made me cry," your sentence will be incorrect. When in doubt about how to use a word, look it up in the dictionary or review **Section 1 on Grammar**.

READER'S VOCABULARY

Homonyms
Homonyms are words that sound the same but have different meanings and spellings. Homonyms can cause writers big problems. Read the following sentences.

>One mourning while weighting four the school bus, I felt a pane in my heal. It seams I had a whole inn my shoe and a peace of glass was cot inside.

See all the mistakes? The writer didn't pay attention to the spelling and meaning of those misused homonyms. The following sentences are correct.

>One morning while waiting for the school bus, I felt a pain in my heel. It seems I had a hole in my shoe and a piece of glass was caught inside.

Here is a list of commonly misused homonyms.

their/there/they're	aunt/ant	stationary/stationery	pail/pale
too/to/two	plane/plain	kernel/colonel	hi/high
your/you're	fare/fair	straight/strait	serial/cereal
its/it's	hall/haul	sight/site/cite	cell/sell
who's/whose	write/right/rite	piece/peace	weak/week
know/no	pear/pair/pare	would/wood	maid/made
feat/feet	rows/rose	steel/steal	main/mane
dew/do/due	toe/tow	grown/groan	lone/loan
week/weak	rowed/road/rode	meet/meat	hear/heard
ate/eight	sow/so/sew	through/threw	break/brake
flower/flour	knew/new	by/bye/buy	great/grate
scent/cent/sent	in/inn	heel/heal	bear/bare
weather/whether	see/sea	deer/dear	cheep/cheap
	sun/son	principal/principle	pair/pare/pear
	blew/blue	where/wear/ware	whole/hole

Homographs

The word *homograph* has two roots: *homo*, which means "the same," and *graph*, which means "write." **Homographs** are words that are written the same, having the same spelling. Homographs are even pronounced the same way sometimes, but they have different meanings. That's because each meaning comes from a different root. Take the word *hatch* for example. *Hatch* can be used to describe a chick coming out of its egg, markings someone has carved on a wall, or a door leading to a ship's cargo area.

> hatch—bring forth young
> hatch—to draw, cut, or engrave fine lines
> hatch—an opening in a ship's deck

Watch out for homographs in your writing. Look them up in a dictionary to be sure you have used these tricky words correctly.

Context Clues

Often you can guess what a word means from the clues given by other words in the sentence. For example, you may never have heard the word *illegible*. But if your teacher says, "I cannot read this paper because your handwriting is illegible," you could guess without the help of a dictionary that *illegible* means "impossible to read." Discovering the meaning of a word by looking at the other words in a sentence is called learning from context. This skill plays an important role in developing a good vocabulary.

Context clues can also help you write a report that any reader will be able to clearly understand. When you use new vocabulary that you have learned while researching your report, be sure to use context clues to define any new concept words you used. For example:

> Many submarines of the Civil War did not have *periscopes*, which allow the drivers to look above the water while the submarine is submerged. As a result, the drivers had to rely on other instruments to figure out where they were going.

Your readers may not know exactly what a *periscope* is, but by using context clues in the sentence, you can help them figure out that it is something used to look above the water.

Concept Words

A **concept word** is a word that has to do with a certain topic or idea. When you write about baseball, you may use the words *base, home run,* and *strike*. These are all baseball concept words. When you write about playing music, you may use the words *key, sharp,* and *time signature*. These are music concept words.

When you write a report about a topic that's new to you, be sure to learn the concept words that will help you explain your topic clearly. When you are researching your topic, look up words you don't know in the dictionary. You can also use the glossary of a book to help you find definitions.

Synonyms and Connotation

Synonyms are words that mean the same thing. *Big* and *large* are synonyms. Sometimes words that are synonyms have different shades of meaning. For example, *slim, skinny, slender,* and *scrawny* are synonyms. But while slim and slender are positive adjectives, *skinny* and *scrawny* give a negative sense of being too thin or ugly. A word's shade of

meaning is called its *connotation.*

Connotation can also be defined as the "feeling" meaning rather than the literal dictionary definition that you get from a word. *Denotation* is the exact dictionary meaning of a word. Pay attention to the connotation, or feeling, of words that you use. When describing a dark and stormy night, you would not use the adjective *fluffy* to describe the clouds. *Fluffy* has a positive connotation. Instead, you could describe the clouds as *jagged, racing,* or *monstrous.* These words have the dark connotation you want.

You can use synonyms to improve your writing. A thesaurus is an excellent source of synonyms. While describing a perfect day, if you find yourself using *beautiful* too many times, a thesaurus will remind you of words like *dazzling* and *sparkling*—words that are more exact and descriptive. When using a thesaurus, beware of choosing a word whose exact meaning you do not understand. For example, *remark* and *yell* are both synonyms for *say,* but they have very different meanings.

Antonyms
Antonyms are words that have opposite meanings. *Tiny* and *huge* are antonyms. Use antonyms in your writing to help you stress an important point. When two things you are describing are very different, use antonyms to describe them. You can find antonyms at the end of thesaurus entries. To find words meaning *unhappy,* you could look up *happy* and find several antonyms such as *sad, melancholy,* or *miserable.*

Sensory Words
Sensory words are words that describe the senses. They explain and describe what a character sees, tastes, hears, smells, or touches. Sensory words are mostly adjectives, adverbs, and verbs. Add sensory words throughout your writing to make scenes more exciting and feelings stronger. Some words are used so often or can have so many different meanings that they do not give exact descriptions. These words usually can be replaced with synonyms that are more exact. When you see overused words in your writing, use a thesaurus to help you replace them with sensory words that are stronger and clearer.

Overused Words

nice	bad	happy	pretty
cute	said	sad	went
good	scary	great	came

Vivid Verbs

absorb	glare	rattle	smack
bolt	inspect	rip	swoop
decline	laud	sandbag	zoom
ebb	peek	scream	
glance	praise	screech	

Adjectives

beaming	deceitful	intriguing	quizzical
beefy	enchanting	inviting	sinister
bulky	engrossing	lustrous	vast
curious	glossy	magnificent	wicked
dark	immense	moldy	

Onomatopoeia

Onomatopoeia is a word that sounds like the sound it describes. Onomatopoeia words are excellent sensory words that add color and interest to your writing. Here is a list of useful onomatopoeia words.

ruff	bark	cluck	clop
clip	drip	murmur	rustle
chirp	clack	oink	howl
neigh	clang	crash	honk
cluck	clatter	snap	hiss
cock-a-doodle-doo	bong	swish	sizzle
moo	blink	smack	burp
baa	zip	smash	buzz
sigh	zoom	squeak	crack
giggle	meow	squeal	
drop	purr	roar	

Prefixes

A **prefix** is one or more syllables added to the beginning of a word to change the word's meaning. Many words have prefixes. By learning the meaning of the most common prefixes, you will be able to add many new words to your vocabulary. Here is list of common prefixes and their meanings.

Prefix	**Meaning**	**Example**
pre	before	prefix, preview
post	after	postpone, postgame
de	from	decide, debate
re	again	recreate, recharge
col	with	collect, collage
com	with	combine, comfort
con	with	concert, connect
mis	wrong	misbehave, misspell
un	not	unclear, untrue
im	not	improper, impossible
in	not, into	inactive, infects
mid	middle	midway, midnight
sub	beneath	submarine, subway
under	below	underneath, underline
semi	half, partly	semicircle, semifinal
super	more than	supernatural, superpower

auto	self	automobile, autobiography
un	not	unhappy, unpleasant
uni	one	unicycle, unicorn
bi	two	bicycle, bilingual
tri	three	tricycle, triangle
quadr	four	quarter, quadrant
pent	five	pentagon
quint	five	quintet
cent	hundred	century, cent

Suffixes

A **suffix** is a syllable, group of syllables, or a word added to the end of a word to change its meaning or part of speech. Here is a list of common suffixes and their meanings.

Suffix	Definition	Example
ist	person who does, makes, or practices	scientist, dentist
less	without or lacking	homeless, jobless
ness	state of quality of being	kindness, likeness
ly	when, how, like, or in the manner of	quietly, calmly
fy	to make or cause to be or become	beautify, purify
ize	to cause to be or become	hypnotize, realize
ion	state or quality of	nation, hibernation
ry	state or quality of	bravery, forgery
ry	place	bakery, grocery
ment	thing	ornament, instrument
ism	state or quality of	heroism, sexism
logy	study or science of	biology, zoology

Root and Base Words

Many words consist of one or more Greek or Latin roots. For example, the Greek root *tele* means "far." When it is combined with *vis*, the Latin root for "see," we get *television*—an invention that lets us *see* pictures coming from *far* away.

Here is a list of Greek and Latin roots. Use this list as a reference to help you use words correctly in your writing.

Greek Number Prefixes

Number	Prefix	Number	Prefix	Number	Prefix
one	mon	six	hexa	eleven	hendeca
two	di, bi	seven	hepta	twelve	dodeca
three	tri	eight	octa	hundred	hecta
four	tetra	nine	ennea		
five	penta	ten	deca		

Greek Prefixes

A-, AN-: without, not:
agnostic, anarchy

ACRO-: a point, topmost, at the tip:
acrobat, acrophobia

ANA-: back, again, according to:
anabolism, anachronism

ANTI-: against:
antibacterial, antidote

APO-: off, away from:
Apocrypha, apostle

AUTO-: self:
autobiography, autocracy

CAT-, CATA-: down, against, mind, remember:
cataclysm, catacomb

DIA-: through, across, over:
diabolic, diagonal

DYS-: ill, bad:
dyslexia, dystopia

ECTO-: without, on the outside:
ectoderm, ectopic (pregnancy)

EN-: in:
encapsulate, endemic

ENDO-: within, internal:
endocrine, endometrium

EPI-: upon, over, at, near:
epicenter, epidermis

ESO-: inward:
esoteric, esotery

EU-: good, well:
eulogy, euphoria

EXO-: outside, external:
exoskeleton, exothermic

HYPER-: over:
hyperactive, hyperbole

HYPO-: under:
hypocritical, hypodermic

MACRO-: large:
macrocosm,
macroglobulin

META-: among, between, changed:
metabolic, metaphysics

MICRO-: small:
microphone, microwave

MISO-, MISA-: hate:
misogyny, misanthrope

PALIN-: back, again:
palindrome, palingenesis

PAN-: all:
panacea, pandemic

PARA-: beside, beyond:
parabolic, parallel

PERI-: around:
perimeter, periphery

POLY-: many:
polygamy, polygon

PSEUD-: false:
pseudepigrapha, pseudonym

SYM-, SYN-: together:
sympathy, synonym

TELE-: at a distance:
telegram, telephone

XENO-: foreign, strange:
xenon, xenophobia

Greek Roots

ANGEL: messenger:
angel, archangel, evangelist

ARCH: to rule, begin:
archangel, monarch, anarchy

ARCH: ancient, old:
archaeology, archaic, archetype

ASTRO, ASTER: star:
astronaut, asterisk, disaster

ATHL: a prize, contest:
athlete, decathlon

ATMO: vapor, gas:
atmometer, atmosphere

BIBLI: book, papyrus, scroll:
bibliography, biblist
(bible)

BIO: life:
biological, autobiography

BLEM, BOL, PARL: to throw:
problem, symbol, diabolic,
parliament

CHROM: color:
chromatic, chromolithography

CHRON: time:
chronology, anachronism

COSM: earth, world:
  cosmic, cosmopolitan
CYCL: cycle, wheel:
  cyclone, bicycle, recyclable
DEM, DEMO, PLEB: the people:
  demagogue, endemic, democracy,
  plebeian
DERM: skin:
  dermatosis, epidermis
DEUTERO: second:
  Deuteronomy, deuteropathy
DICHO: in two parts:
  dichogamous, dichotomy
DIPLO: double:
  diploid, diplopod
DOX: to praise, worship:
  doxology, orthodox
  (dogma)
DROME: to run:
  dromedary, palindrome
DYNA: force, power, strength:
  dynamic, dynasty
ECO: ecology:
  ecosystem, ecotype
ELECTRO: electric:
  electrolyte, electromagnetic
ERG, URG: work:
  energy, surgeon
ETHNO: race, nation:
  ethnocentrism, ethnography
GAM, GAMY: marriage:
  bigamist, polygamy
GEO: earth:
  geographic, geology
GNOS: to know:
  Gnosticism, agnostic, diagnosis
  (physiognomy)
GRAM, GRAPH: write:
  gramophone, telegram, graphic,
  autograph, autobiography
HELIO: sun:
  heliocentric, heliotrope
  (helium)
HETERO: different:
  heterogeneous, heterologous

HOMO, HOMEO: same:
  homosapien, homeopathic
HYDR: water:
  hydrate, hydraulic
IDO: form, shape:
  idol, kaleidoscope
  (idyll)
LEXI, LOG, LOGUE: word, to speak:
  lexicographer, dyslexia, catalog,
  dialogue
LITH: stone:
  lithography, Paleolithic
LOG, LOGY: word, study of:
  logic, biological,
  chronology
MAT, METRO: mother:
  matrimony, metropolitan
METRO: measure:
  metrology, metronome
NAU: ship:
  nausea, astronaut
NECRO: corpse:
  necrophilia, necropsy
OD: way, journey:
  period, episode
ONYM: a name:
  acronym, patronymic
  (onomatopoeia)
OSTEO: bone:
  osteopath, osteoporosis
PALEO: ancient, old:
  Paleolithic, paleontology
PATH: to suffer:
  pathology, sociopath,
  homeopathic
PATRO: father:
  patronize, patronymic
PED: child:
  pediatrics, orthopedic
PHIL: love:
  philosopher, necrophilia
PHOB: fear:
  phobia, acrophobia
PHON: sound:
  phonics, microphone

PHOTO: light:
   photocopy, photography
PHYS: nature:
   physics, physiology
POD: foot:
   podiatry, tripod
POLI: city:
   police, politics, cosmopolitan,
   metropolis
PSYCH: mind:
   psychology, psychosis
PYR: fire:
   pyre, pyromaniac
SCHIZO: split:
   schizoid, schizophrenia
SCOPE: see, look at:
   horoscope, microscope
   (bishop)
   (episcopal)

SOPH: wisdom:
   sophisticate, philosopher
THE: a god:
   theology, atheism, pantheon
THERM: heat:
   thermoelectric, thermostat
THES: to put, place:
   thesis, antithesis
   (apothecary)
TOM, TOMY: to cut:
   atom, appendectomy
TOP: a place:
   topic, utopia
TRI: three:
   triangle, tripod
ZOO: animal:
   zoo, zoology

Greek Suffixes

–AST: one associated with:
   enthusiast, gymnast
–IA: pathological condition, territory,
   pertaining to:
   malaria, Romania
–ICS: thing having to do with:
   ethics, politics
–ISM: action, condition, doctrine:
   barbarism, criticism

–IST: makes, advocates:
   apologist, socialist
–ITE: native, adherent, a part of
   a body, rock/mineral:
   Israelite, sulfite
–OID: resembling:
   factoid, humanoid

Latin Numbers

Number	Prefix	Number	Prefix	Number	Prefix
zero	nihil	five	quinque	ten	decem
one	una	six	sex	hundred	centum
two	duo	seven	septem	thousand	mille
three	tres	eight	octo		
four	quattuor	nine	novem		

Latin Prefixes

AB–: from, by:
   abdicate, abduct
AMBI–: around, about:
   ambidextrous, ambiguous
ANTE–: before:
   antebellum, antecedent

BENE–, BENI–: good, well:
   benediction, benign
CIRCUM–: around:
   circumcise, circumference
CO–, COM–: together:
   coalition, communist

CONTRA–: against, facing:
   contraband, contradict
DE–: down, away, off, utterly:
   debase, descendant
DIS–: otherwise, apart:
   disable, disconnect
EX–: out, off, away, thoroughly:
   example, expatriate
EXTRA–: outside:
   extracurricular, extradite
IN–, IM–, EN–: in, into, on:
   inquest, important, enchant
IN–, IL–, IM–, IR–: not:
   infinite, illogical, impartial, irreverent
INFRA–: below, beneath, inferior to:
   infrasonic, infrastructure
INTER–: between:
   interact, intermural
INTRA–: within:
   intramural, intravenous
JUXTA–: near, beside:
   juxtapose, juxtaposit
MAGNI–: great, large:
   magnificent, magnify
MULTI–: many:
   multicultural, multifaceted
NE–, NON–: not:
   negate, nonchalant

OB–: toward, across, opposite:
   object, obverse
PER–: through, by means of:
   percent, perennial
POST–: after:
   postdate, postpartum
PRE–: before:
   prejudice, president
PRO–: in favor of, forward, instead of, before:
   prodemocracy, prologue
RE–: again, back:
   reactor, realign
RETRO–: backward:
   retroactive, retrograde
   (retreat)
SE–: aside, apart:
   seclude, secret
SEMI–: half:
   semiannual, semicolon
SUB–: beneath, secretly:
   subterfuge, subterranean
SUPER–: above:
   superfluous, superior
TRANS–: across, over:
   transcend, transfer

Latin Roots

ACT, GATE, GEN, GI, GU: to act, do, drive:
   actual, enact, reactor, fumigate,
   agenda, agitate, ambiguous
AERO: air, gas:
   aerodynamics, aerosol
AL: to feed, nourish, grow:
   alimentary, coalition
   (adolescence)
   (adulthood)
AMA, AMO: to love:
   amateur, amorous, enamored
ANIM: mind, soul:
   animate, equanimity
ANNI, ANNU, ENNI: year:
   anniversary, annual, semiannual,
   perennial

BAT: to beat:
   battery, acrobat, debate
CAD, CAS, CID: to fall:
   cadaver, decadence, casualty,
   occasion, accident, coincide
CAL, CHA: to be warm, hot:
   calorie, scalding, nonchalant
CANT, CHANT: to sing:
   cantata, descant, incantation,
   chant, enchant
   (accent)
   (incentive)
**CAP, CAPT, CAS, CHAS, CEIT, CEIV,
CEPT, CIP, CUP:** to seize, lay hold of,
   contain:
   capable, captive, case, chase,

conceit, deceive, accept, anticipate, occupy

CENTRI: center:
centrifuge, centripetal (force)

CIT, CIV: citizen:
city, civil

CLOS, CLUDE, CLUS: to shut, close:
closet, conclude, exclusive
(claustrophobia)
(cloister)

COGN, GNOR, NOTI: to get to know:
cognitive, recognize, ignore, notice
(acquaintance)

CRED: to believe, trust:
credible, accredited
(creed)
(grant)
(miscreant)

DAT, DIT: to give:
data, edit, tradition
(traitor)
(rendezvous)
(vendor)

DEXT: on the right, skillful:
dexterity, ambidextrous

DIC: to tell, to say:
dictator, benediction, contradict, judicial
(judge)

DISCI: to learn:
disciple, discipline

DOC: to teach:
doctor, document

DON: to give:
donate, pardon, condone

DOU, DUB, DUO, DUP: two:
doubt, indubitably, duo, duplicate
(dual)
(duet)

EAS, JAC, JECT, JET: to lie, throw:
easy, adjacent, reject, trajectory, jettisoned

EGO: I:
egocentric, egotistic

ERR: to wander:
erratic, aberrant

EV: age:
longevity, medieval

FAC, FACE, FACT, FEAS, FEAT, FECT, FEIT, FIT, FIC, FICE: to make, do:
faculty, surface, fact, feasible, feature, refectory, forfeit, profit, artificial, sacrifice

FER: to bear, bring, carry:
fertile, transfer, circumference

FLU: to flow:
fluorescent, influenza

FORM: form, shape:
formula, conform, reformatory

GEN: race, kind:
gender, general

GRAC, GRAT, GREE: beloved, dear, pleasing:
grace, gratuity, agree

GRAD, GRESS: to go, step, walk:
grade, biodegradable, congress, aggression

IT: to go:
itinerate, circuit, ambitious
(ambience)
(errant)
(perishable)

JUR, JUS: to swear:
jury, perjure, justice

LAT: carried, borne:
latitude, legislator

LEG: law:
legislator, privilege

LEV: to lighten, lift, raise:
lever, elevate

LITER: letter of the alphabet:
literature, alliterate

LONG: long:
longevity, prolong, elongated

MAN: hand:
manipulate, manual

MAN: to remain:
mansion, permanent
(remain)

MED: middle:
median, medieval
(mean)
(middle)

MISE, MISS, MIT, MITT: to send:
  compromise, mission, dismiss,
  admit, permitted
NOM: name:
  nomenclature, denomination
OMNI: all:
  omnipotent, omnivore
PAR, EQU: equal, peer:
  par, comparison, equanimity
PAR: to give birth to, come in sight:
  parent, postpartum
PATRI: father:
  patriarch, patriot
  (paternoster)
PED: foot:
  pedigree, biped, centipede
  (impeach)
PEL, PUL: to drive:
  pelt, propel, pulse, compulsive
PEN, PEND, PENS, POND: to weigh, hang, pay:
  pensive, pendant, depend,
  pension, dispense, ponder
PORT: to carry:
  report, transport, important
PUN, PUNC: to point, stab:
  pun, punctuate, compunction
  (poignant)
  (point)
QUEST, QUIR, QUIS: to seek:
  quest, inquest, inquire, prerequisite
QUI: quiet, rest:
  quit, requiem
ROG: to ask:
  rogue, derogatory, interrogate
SAL, SULT/XULT: to leap, spring forward:
  salmon, result, exultation
SCEN, SCEND: to climb, leap:
  descendant, ascend, condescend
  (scan)
SCI: to know:
  science, conscious, omniscient
SCRI: to write:
  scripture, describe, postscript

SECU/XECU, SEQU, SUIT: to follow:
  consecutive, execute, sequel,
  pursuit
  (sect)
  (segue)
  (intrinsic)
SED, SESS, SID: to sit, settle:
  sediment, session, possess,
  president, reside
  (hostage)
SEMBL, SIMIL, SIMUL: like, at the same time:
  assemble, similar, simulate
SEN: old, old man:
  senate, senile
SEN, SENT: to be, exist:
  absence, present
SIGN: a mark, seal, sign:
  signature, assign, designate
SOL: alone:
  solo, desolate
SOL: sun:
  solar, insolate
SON, SOUND: to sound:
  sonar, resound
TEMP: time:
  temporary, extemporaneous
TERR, TERRA: earth, land:
  territory, terrarium, mediterranean
ULT: last, beyond, extremely:
  ultimate, penultimate
  (outrageous)
USE, UTI: to use:
  use, abuse, utilize
VIT, VIV: to live:
  vitamin, vivid, survive
  (viable)
VOC, VOK: to call, voice:
  vocation, advocate, invoke
VOR: to devour:
  voracious, carnivorous

Latin Suffixes

-ACIOUS: tending to:
audacious, bodacious

-CLE, -CULUM: means, instrument, place:
particle, curriculum

-ILE: relating to, capable of:
docile, fragile

-ION: the act or result of, state or process:
hydration, oxidation

-IUM: the act, something connected with the act:
equilibrium, solarium

-MENT: result or means of an act:
adornment, advancement

-OR: act or condition of, one who performs an action:
accelerator, squalor

Imported Words

Imported words are English words that come from other languages, such as French, Arabic, or Japanese. Like Latin and Greek roots, many imported words have been used in the English language for a very long time. Many dictionaries give an etymology, or short word history, to tell what language a word comes from originally. Here is a list of commonly used imported words.

catalogue	toboggan	July	museum
carrousel	Texas	August	hypnosis
boulevard	Michigan	September	panic
question	pecan	October	jovial
bouquet	Alabama	November	titanic
budget	hickory	December	comrade
crayon	Alaska	Sunday	caravan
menu	raccoon	Monday	bungalow
lieu	moccasin	Tuesday	scant
bandage	January	Wednesday	solo
rare	February	Thursday	clan
cinema	March	Friday	asphalt
tepee	April	Saturday	
opossum	May	cereal	
Canada	June	geology	

Compound Words

Compound words are words made up of two or more base words. They can be written as one word, two words, or with a hyphen to connect them. Compound words can take the place of a long explanation and make a statement clearer.

Ben was happy to meet his *mom's new husband's son* for the first time.

Ben was happy to meet his *stepbrother* for the first time.

WRITER'S VOCABULARY

Literal v. Figurative Speech

When people say something that you know is untrue but is being said to make a point, you say they are using a **figure of speech**. Authors use figurative language to make their writing more interesting.

I was so hungry I could have eaten an elephant.

When people say something true, they are speaking **literally**. They are saying exactly what they mean.

I was so hungry I ate a bowl of hot soup and a cheese sandwich.

Idioms

An **idiom** is a phrase that has a non-literal, or figurative, meaning. Non-literal means that the words in the phrase, when understood by their dictionary meanings, do not literally mean what the phrase says. For example, *caught a cold* is an idiom. The speaker did not literally run around with a net until he or she caught the cold. The speaker means he or she got a cold.

It is fine to use idioms in your informal or fiction writing. But avoid idioms in your formal, non-fiction writing. People who speak English as their second language do not know idioms as well as native speakers, and idioms can be hard to learn. In formal writing, you want everyone who picks up your paper to be able to read it. Your reader may have trouble if you've used a lot of idioms. Here is a list of common idioms to avoid.

pull a fast one
do the honors
for the birds
cost an arm and a leg
caught a cold
ahead of time
drop me a line
in the same boat
take the rap
lose your temper

get away with it
get the picture
get up on the wrong side
   of the bed
really opened my eyes
the writing's on the wall
make ends meet
give your right arm
see eye to eye
on the ball

burn up
blow out
get lost
pull through
hang out
keep your head up
go back on your word
turn the tables

Clichés

A **cliché** is an overused phrase or idea, such as "early to bed, early to rise makes a man healthy, wealthy, and wise." Avoid clichés at all cost. These phrases are old and tired and because they've been around so long, they make your writing unclear. Replace clichés with words that say what you really mean. Here is a list of clichés to avoid.

If you can't beat them, join them.
Actions speak louder than words.
Absence makes the heart grow fonder.
Don't count your chickens before they've hatched.
The early bird catches the worm.

Waste not, want not.
Beggars can't be choosers.
Look before you leap.
You can't have your cake and eat it too.
Like father, like son.
A rolling stone gathers no moss.
A picture is worth a thousand words.
Every cloud has a silver lining.

Imagery

Once you understand the idea behind figurative language, you will be able to understand **imagery** as well. *Imagery* comes from the root word *image*, which means *picture*—something you can see. When you write using the device of imagery, you write so vividly and creatively that readers can see what you are writing in their imaginations.

Simile and Metaphor

Metaphors and **similes** are comparisons that are made for color or emphasis. Similes use *like* or *as* to compare two unrelated things. Metaphors do not use *like* or *as* but make a direct comparison.

> **simile:** The cat looked like a carved statue.
> **metaphor:** The fog was a gray blanket that lay over the town.

Symbolism

A **symbol** is a literal thing, place, or happening in writing that has a figurative meaning.

> Leaving the bright daylight of the May afternoon, he entered the gloomy darkness of the piano teacher's parlor. Another week had passed, and Bob still hadn't been practicing.

In the first sentence, *light* can symbolize peace of mind, while the *darkness* and *gloom* can symbolize the uncertainty and anxiousness Bob feels because he hasn't prepared for his lesson. Writers use symbolism to add depth to their writing. Instead of telling you that Bob feels anxious or uncertain, the writer shows you by using symbolism.

Personification

Personification is exactly what it sounds like—giving an inanimate object, like a rock or a chair, human qualities.

> Dressed in its best, glowing from head to toe, and standing perfectly straight and tall, the old house seemed brand new as it welcomed Susan in from the cold.

Sound Devices

Because there are fewer words in a poem than in a story, every word in poetry is important. By writing or arranging words in a certain way, the author makes words and phrases sound a certain way to set the tone of the poem.

Onomatopoeia is a term for words that sound like the sound they describe. Buzz, pop, snap, and fizz are all words displaying onomatopoeia.

Alliteration is a sound device, too. Starting every word in a phrase with the same letter is

alliteration. Using a soft sound like *s* makes a poem feel gentle. Using harsher tones like *k* or *r* make a poem sound tougher.

>Shining sun shone down on Susan as she sowed her sapling seed.

Assonance is like alliteration. Every word in a phrase starts with a similar vowel sound.

>The always awful authors often arrive on time.

Comparison and Contrast

To set two objects or ideas apart, compare or contrast them. To compare, list reasons why the two things are the same. Choose the strongest connection and circle it. To contrast, list reasons why the two things are different. Choose the strongest contrast and circle it. Then use these comparisons and contrasts in your writing.

An **oxymoron** is a figure of speech in which contrasting terms are put next to each other.

>There was a *deafening silence*.
>The party was a *sad celebration*.
>Jake was a *cold* person with a *warm* heart.

Comparison and contrast can be especially helpful in developing characters. When two characters are very different, show that difference with a point of contrast. When they are very similar, use a comparison to draw your reader's attention to this fact.

Rhyme Schemes

The word *scheme* means *pattern*, so a **rhyme scheme** is a pattern of rhyme used in a poem. How to use rhyme is up to the poet. For that reason, there are many different types of rhyme schemes.

When two lines that appear back to back rhyme, they are called a **couplet**.

>The light of sunset on the bay
>Always takes my cares away.

When there are four lines, and the first line rhymes with the third and the second rhymes with the fourth, it is an **a-b-a-b** pattern rhyme.

>One day in May
>While by the sea
>I ran away
>When you looked at me

Poetry can also be written in **free verse**. Free verse is poetry that doesn't rhyme or follow a specific rhyme scheme. The author writes freely.

>This is a free verse
>So it doesn't have to rhyme
>I can say what I want
>Without worrying about it.

APPENDIX I: THE NEWBERY MEDAL

The Newbery Medals honor achievement in children's writing. Each year, a winner is announced. Here is a complete list of Newbery winners. To find out more about the award, visit the American Library Association's website at http://www.ala.org/alsc/newbery.html.

2003: *Crispin: The Cross of Lead* by Avi (Hyperion Press)
2002: *A Single Shard* by Linda Sue Park (Clarion Books/Houghton Mifflin)
2001: *A Year Down Yonder* by Richard Peck (Dial)
2000: *Bud, Not Buddy* by Christopher Paul Curtis (Delacorte)
1999: *Holes* by Louis Sachar (Frances Foster)
1998: *Out of the Dust* by Karen Hesse (Scholastic)
1997: *The View from Saturday* by E.L. Konigsburg (Jean Karl/Atheneum)
1996: *The Midwife's Apprentice* by Karen Cushman (Clarion)
1995: *Walk Two Moons* by Sharon Creech (HarperCollins)
1994: *The Giver* by Lois Lowry (Houghton)
1993: *Missing May* by Cynthia Rylant (Jackson/Orchard)
1992: *Shiloh* by Phyllis Reynolds Naylor (Atheneum)
1991: *Maniac Magee* by Jerry Spinelli (Little, Brown)
1990: *Number the Stars* by Lois Lowry (Houghton)
1989: *Joyful Noise: Poems for Two Voices* by Paul Fleischman (Harper)
1988: *Lincoln: A Photobiography* by Russell Freedman (Clarion)
1987: *The Whipping Boy* by Sid Fleischman (Greenwillow)
1986: *Sarah, Plain and Tall* by Patricia MacLachlan (Harper)
1985: *The Hero and the Crown* by Robin McKinley (Greenwillow)
1984: *Dear Mr. Henshaw* by Beverly Cleary (Morrow)
1983: *Dicey's Song* by Cynthia Voigt (Atheneum)
1982: *A Visit to William Blake's Inn: Poems for Innocent and Experienced Travelers* by Nancy Willard (Harcourt)
1981: *Jacob Have I Loved* by Katherine Paterson (Crowell)
1980: *A Gathering of Days: A New England Girl's Journal, 1830-1832* by Joan W. Blos (Scribner)
1979: *The Westing Game* by Ellen Raskin (Dutton)
1978: *Bridge to Terabithia* by Katherine Paterson (Crowell)
1977: *Roll of Thunder, Hear My Cry* by Mildred D. Taylor (Dial)
1976: *The Grey King* by Susan Cooper (McElderry/Atheneum)
1975: *M. C. Higgins, the Great* by Virginia Hamilton (Macmillan)
1974: *The Slave Dancer* by Paula Fox (Bradbury)
1973: *Julie of the Wolves* by Jean Craighead George (Harper)
1972: *Mrs. Frisby and the Rats of NIMH* by Robert C. O'Brien (Atheneum)
1971: *Summer of the Swans* by Betsy Byars (Viking)
1970: *Sounder* by William H. Armstrong (Harper)
1969: *The High King* by Lloyd Alexander (Holt)
1968: *From the Mixed-Up Files of Mrs. Basil E. Frankweiler* by E. L. Konigsburg (Atheneum)

1967: *Up a Road Slowly* by Irene Hunt (Follett)

1966: *I, Juan de Pareja* by Elizabeth Borton de Trevino (Farrar)

1965: *Shadow of a Bull* by Maia Wojciechowska (Atheneum)

1964: *It's Like This, Cat* by Emily Neville (Harper)

1963: *A Wrinkle in Time* by Madeleine L'Engle (Farrar)

1962: *The Bronze Bow* by Elizabeth George Speare (Houghton)

1961: *Island of the Blue Dolphins* by Scott O'Dell (Houghton)

1960: *Onion John* by Joseph Krumgold (Crowell)

1959: *The Witch of Blackbird Pond* by Elizabeth George Speare (Houghton)

1958: *Rifles for Watie* by Harold Keith (Crowell)

1957: *Miracles on Maple Hill* by Virginia Sorenson (Harcourt)

1956: *Carry On, Mr. Bowditch* by Jean Lee Latham (Houghton)

1955: *The Wheel on the School* by Meindert DeJong (Harper)

1954: *...And Now Miguel* by Joseph Krumgold (Crowell)

1953: *Secret of the Andes* by Ann Nolan Clark (Viking)

1952: *Ginger Pye* by Eleanor Estes (Harcourt)

1951: *Amos Fortune, Free Man* by Elizabeth Yates (Dutton)

1950: *The Door in the Wall* by Marguerite de Angeli (Doubleday)

1949: *King of the Wind* by Marguerite Henry (Rand McNally)

1948: *The Twenty-One Balloons* by William Pène du Bois (Viking)

1947: *Miss Hickory* by Carolyn Sherwin Bailey (Viking)

1946: *Strawberry Girl* by Lois Lenski (Lippincott)

1945: *Rabbit Hill* by Robert Lawson (Viking)

1944: *Johnny Tremain* by Esther Forbes (Houghton)

1943: *Adam of the Road* by Elizabeth Janet Gray (Viking)

1942: *The Matchlock Gun* by Walter Edmonds (Dodd)

1941: *Call It Courage* by Armstrong Sperry (Macmillan)

1940: *Daniel Boone* by James Daugherty (Viking)

1939: *Thimble Summer* by Elizabeth Enright (Rinehart)

1938: *The White Stag* by Kate Seredy (Viking)

1937: *Roller Skates* by Ruth Sawyer (Viking)

1936: *Caddie Woodlawn* by Carol Ryrie Brink (Macmillan)

1935: *Dobry* by Monica Shannon (Viking)

1934: *Invincible Louisa: The Story of the Author of Little Women* by Cornelia Meigs (Little, Brown)

1933: *Young Fu of the Upper Yangtze* by Elizabeth Lewis (Winston)

1932: *Waterless Mountain* by Laura Adams Armer (Longmans)

1931: *The Cat Who Went to Heaven* by Elizabeth Coatsworth (Macmillan)

1930: *Hitty, Her First Hundred Years* by Rachel Field (Macmillan)

1929: *The Trumpeter of Krakow* by Eric P. Kelly (Macmillan)

1928: *Gay Neck, the Story of a Pigeon* by Dhan Gopal Mukerji (Dutton)

1927: *Smoky, the Cowhorse* by Will James (Scribner)

1926: *Shen of the Sea* by Arthur Bowie Chrisman (Dutton)

1925: *Tales from Silver Lands* by Charles Finger (Doubleday)

1924: *The Dark Frigate* by Charles Hawes (Little, Brown)

1923: *The Voyages of Doctor Dolittle* by Hugh Lofting (Lippincott)

1922: *The Story of Mankind* by Hendrik Willem van Loon (Liveright)

APPENDIX 2: PROOFREADER'S MARKS

Proofreader's marks can be used to correct sentences and paragraphs. Here are the most frequently used marks.

Symbol	Meaning	Example
⌗	new paragraph	Many children have lived in the White House.
≡	capital letter	Theodore roosevelt's family may have been the most spirited bunch.
/	lowercase letter	His son, Quentin, once snuck a Pony inside!
∧	insert	Why did Quentin do that? He wanted to cheer up his brother.
ℰ	delete (take out)	Theodore Roosevelt has had six children.
⊙	add a period	Archie and Quentin were the youngest.
⌄	add an apostrophe	Alice was Theodore Roosevelt's oldest child.
⌄	add a comma	Some people thought Alice was too wild, and they criticized Roosevelt.
⌄⌄	add quotation marks	He responded, "I can be president, or I can supervise Alice. Nobody could do both."
∼	transpose (reverse)	The Roosevelt kids had fun in the White House.
⌐	move	They slid on silver trays down the stairs.
•••	stet (leave it as is)	They walked through the hallways on stilts.
#	insert space	The president even played sometimes.
◡	close up space	He liked Hide-and- Seek and pillow fights!

114

APPENDIX 3: THE WRITING PROCESS

1. Prewriting: Think
- Decide on a topic to write about.
- Consider who will read or listen to your written work.
- Brainstorm ideas about the subject.
- List places where you can research information.
- Do your research.

2. Drafting: Write
- Put the information you researched into your own words.
- Write sentences and paragraphs even if they are not perfect.
- Read what you have written and judge if it says what you mean.
- Show it to others and ask for suggestions.

3. Revising: Make it Better
- Read what you have written again.
- Think about what others said about it.
- Rearrange words or sentences.
- Take out or add parts.
- Replace overused or unclear words.
- Read your writing aloud to be sure it flows smoothly.

4. Proofreading: Make it Correct
- Be sure all sentences are complete.
- Correct spelling, capitalization, and punctuation.
- Change words that are not used correctly.
- Have someone check your work.
- Recopy it correctly and neatly.

5. Publishing: Share the Finished Product
- Read your writing aloud to a group.
- Create a book of your work.
- Send a copy to a friend or relative.
- Put your writing on display.
- Illustrate, perform, or set your creation to music.
- Congratulate yourself on a job well done!

APPENDIX 4: THE DEWEY SYSTEM—THE 100 DIVISIONS

000 Generalities
010 Bibliography
020 Library and information sciences
030 General encyclopedic words
040 (Unassigned)
050 General serial publications
060 General organizations and museology
070 Journalism, publishing, newspapers
080 General collections
090 Manuscripts and book rarities

100 Philosophy
110 Metaphysics
120 Epistemology, causation, humankind
130 Paranormal phenomena and arts
140 Specific philosophical viewpoints
150 Psychology
160 Logic
170 Ethics (moral philosophy)
180 Ancient, medieval, Eastern
190 Modern Western philosophy

200 Religion
210 Natural religion
220 Bible
230 Christian theology
240 Christian moral and devotional
250 Local church and religious orders
260 Social and ecclesiastical theology
270 History and geography of church
280 Christian denominations and sects
290 Other and comparative religions

300 Social Sciences
310 Statistics
320 Political science
330 Economics
340 Law
350 Public administration
360 Social problems and services
370 Education
380 Commerce (trade)
390 Customs, etiquette, folklore

400 Language
410 Linguistics
420 English and Anglo-Saxon languages
430 Germanic languages, German
440 Romance languages, French
450 Italian, Romanian, Rhaeto-Romantic
460 Spanish and Portuguese languages
470 Italic languages, Latin
480 Hellenic languages, Classical Greek
490 Other languages

500 Pure Sciences
510 Mathematics
520 Astronomy and allied sciences
530 Physics
540 Chemistry and allied sciences
550 Science or earth and other worlds
560 Paleontology, Paleozoology
570 Life sciences
580 Botanical sciences
590 Zoological sciences

600 Technology (Applied Sciences)
610 Medical sciences, Medicine
620 Engineering and allied operations
630 Agriculture and related technologies
640 Home economics and family living
650 Management and auxiliary services
660 Chemical and related technologies
670 Manufacturers
680 Manufacture for specific uses
690 Buildings

700 The Arts
710 Civic and landscape art
720 Architecture
730 Plastic arts, Sculpture
740 Drawing, decorative and minor arts
750 Painting and paintings
760 Graphic arts, Prints
770 Photography and photographs
780 Music
790 Recreational and performing arts

800 Literature
810 American literature in English
820 English and Anglo-Saxon literatures
830 Literature of Germanic languages
840 Literature of Romance languages
850 Italian, Romanian, Rhaeto-Romantic
860 Spanish and Portuguese literature
870 Italic literature, Latin
880 Hellenic literatures, Greek
890 Literatures of other languages

900 Geography and History
910 General geography, travel
920 General biography and genealogy
930 General history of ancient world
940 General history of Europe
950 General history of Asia
960 General history of Africa
970 General history of North America
980 General history of South America
990 General history of other areas

APPENDIX 5: ABBREVIATIONS

Abbreviations are shortened versions of a word used to save space. Abbreviations are often used on dates, invitations, directions and street maps, and measurements. Here is a list of commonly used abbreviations.

Sun.	Sunday		Blvd.	boulevard
Mon.	Monday		Hwy.	highway
Tues.	Tuesday		Pl.	place
Wed.	Wednesday		Ln.	lane
Thurs.	Thursday		Ct.	court
Fri.	Friday		mph	miles per hour
Sat.	Saturday			
			in.	inch
Jan.	January		ft.	foot
Feb.	February		yd.	yard
Mar.	March		mi.	mile
Apr.	April		mm	millimeter
May			cm	centimeter
June			m	meter
July			km	kilometer
Aug.	August		pt.	pint
Sept.	September		qt.	quart
Oct.	October		gal.	gallon
Nov.	November		oz.	ounce
Dec.	December		lb.	pound
			tsp.	teaspoon
Rd.	road		TBSP.	tablespoon
St.	street		c.	cup

Abbreviations are also used on titles before and after people's names, names of countries, dates, familiar organizations, and public services.

Dr.	doctor		A.D.	Anno Domini (in the year of our Lord)
Mr.	mister		a.m.	ante meridiem (morning)
Mrs.	missus		p.m.	post meridiem (afternoon)
Ms.	mademoiselle		sec.	second
Ph. D.	doctor of philosophy		min.	minute
M.D.	medical doctor		hr.	hour
Jr.	junior		wk.	week
Sr.	senior		mo.	month
			yr.	year
USA	United States of America			
			org.	organization
B.C.	before Christ		govt.	government
B.C.E.	before Common Era		univ.	university

pres.	president	misc.	miscellaneous
v.p.	vice president	etc.	et cetera
dept.	department	ea.	each
		e.g.	for example

Postal Abbreviations and Possession Abbreviations

States

AL	Alabama	NM	New Mexico
AK	Alaska	NY	New York
AZ	Arizona	NC	North Carolina
AR	Arkansas	ND	North Dakota
CA	California	OH	Ohio
CO	Colorado	OK	Oklahoma
CT	Connecticut	OR	Oregon
DE	Delaware	PA	Pennsylvania
FL	Florida	RI	Rhode Island
GA	Georgia	SC	South Carolina
HI	Hawaii	SD	South Dakota
ID	Idaho	TN	Tennessee
IL	Illinois	TX	Texas
IN	Indiana	UT	Utah
IA	Iowa	VT	Vermont
KS	Kansas	VA	Virginia
KY	Kentucky	WA	Washington
LA	Louisiana	WV	West Virginia
ME	Maine	WI	Wisconsin
MD	Maryland	WY	Wyoming
MA	Massachusetts		
MI	Michigan	DC	District of Columbia
MN	Minnesota		
MS	Mississippi		**U.S. Possessions**
MO	Missouri	AS	American Samoa
MT	Montana	GU	Guam
NE	Nebraska	PR	Puerto Rico
NV	Nevada	VI	Virgin Islands
NH	New Hampshire		
NJ	New Jersey		

GLOSSARY

A

abbreviation: the shortening of a word

abstract noun: a noun that names an idea or concept

act: divides the action of a play

action verb: a verb that tells what someone or something did, is doing, or will do

active voice: when the subject performs the action of the verb

adjective: a word that describes what kind, which one, or how many of a noun or pronoun

adverb: a word that modifies a verb, an adjective, or another adverb by telling how, when, where, or how often

adverb clause: a dependent clause that functions as an adverb, modifying verbs, adjectives, or other adverbs and telling where, when, in what manner, to what extent, under what condition, or why

alliteration: a sound device; the author starts most of the words in a phrase or sentence with the same consonant sound

almanac: a reference book that contains facts on many subjects, including government, history, sports, and entertainment

alphabetical order: listing materials in ABC order

antecedent: the noun that a pronoun refers to or replaces

antonyms: words that mean the opposite

apostrophe: a punctuation mark used to show possession, or to mark the place of missing letters in a contraction

appendix: a section at the back of a book that gives more information about a specific topic

appositive: a noun or noun phrase placed next to or very near another noun or noun phrase to identify, explain, or supplement its meaning or to rename the initial noun or pronoun.

article: the words *a, an,* and *the* used as special adjectives that describe a singular noun

assonance: a sound device; the author starts most of the words in a phrase or sentence with the same vowel sound

atlas: a reference book of maps

audience: people who will read your writing

audio-visual: music or video sources

author's group: group of writers who share their writing and discuss it

autobiography: the story of a person's life told by that person

B

base word: a word that can stand on its own without prefixes or suffixes

bibliography: an alphabetical listing of authors, titles, and publication information for each source used in a book or piece of writing

biography: the story of a person's life not written by that person

body: the main text, apart from the introduction or conclusion, in a report, essay, story, or letter

brackets: punctuation marks used in quotations to separate extra words or explanations from the quote

brainstorm: write ideas, questions, things you know, and things you want to know to help you get ideas for your paper and to narrow a topic that interests you

business letter: a formal letter written to make a suggestion or request of a business person

C

capitalization: use a capital letter at the beginning of a sentence, on a proper noun, and in titles

characters: the people, animals, or things to whom the action happens in a story

checklist: a list of ways to improve writing, including word usage and punctuation

chronological: time order; ordering events by when they took place in time

cinquain: a five line poem about a thing that follows a specific pattern

cliché: an overused, idiomatic phrase

closing: the way the writer says good-bye in a letter

clues: elements of a mystery story that the narrator or main character uses to solve the crime

collective noun: a word that names a group of people, places, or things

colon: a punctuation mark used to separate a series from a sentence, to indicate the break between hours and minutes in the time, and to follow a salutation in a business letter

comma: a punctuation mark used to indicate a pause in or break in a sentence, phrase, or clause

common noun: a word that names any person, place, or thing

comparative adjective: an adjective that describes a comparison between two things, people, places, or actions

comparative adverb: an adverb that describes a comparison between two things, people, places, or actions

complete predicate: all the words in the sentence that describe what the subject is doing, did, or will do

complete subject: all the words in the sentence that describe what or who is being talked about

complex sentence: a type of sentence that contains an independent clause and one or more dependent clauses

compound complex sentence: a type of sentence that contains two or more independent clauses and at least one dependent clause

compound predicate: two or more predicates that have the same subject and are joined by a conjunction

compound sentence: a type of sentence that contains two independent clauses that are closely related

compound subject: two or more subjects that have the same verb and are joined by a conjunction

compound word: two or more words written together as one word, two words, or connected by hyphens

concept words: vocabulary words that have to do with a certain topic

concrete noun: a word that names something that can be seen or touched

concrete poem: a poem written around or on a picture of an object

conjunction: a word that connects words or phrases

connotation: the feeling meaning of a word; a word's shade of meaning

context clues: clues within a sentence that help you define unknown words

contraction: a combination of two words that has an apostrophe to take the place of any removed letters

coordinating conjunction: a conjunction that coordinates, or organizes, the connection between two independent clauses

copyright page: the page following the title page that tells where and when the book was published

couplet: two lines of rhyming poetry

D

dangling modifier: a modifying word, phrase, or clause that does not modify a particular word

dash: a punctuation mark used to separate parts of a sentence

declarative sentence: a type of sentence that makes a statement

demonstrative adjective: an adjective that modifies a noun by telling which one or which ones

demonstrative pronoun: a pronoun that shows which noun is being talked about in the sentence

denotation: the dictionary definition of a word

dependent clause: a clause that cannot stand alone and depends upon the independent clause of the sentence to complete its meaning

Dewey Decimal System: system of cataloguing non-fiction books created by librarian Melvil Dewey in 1876

dialogue: the conversation between two characters in a story

dictionary: a book containing an alphabetical listing of words and their parts of speech, definitions, origins, spellings, and pronunciations

direct object: a noun or pronoun that answers the question, "what?" or "whom?" after the verb

direct quotation: the exact words of a character or author in quotation marks

drafting: the second part of the writing process; writing the first draft of the paper

double negative: using two negative words (such as *not, neither, hardly*) in the same sentence

double-space: writing or typing text with a line of space between every written line

E

ellipsis points: a punctuation mark used to mark the place of words removed from a quotation

encyclopedia: a collection of alphabetical volumes containing general facts and statistics about many topics

encyclopedia index: a separate volume that lists all the places where information on a certain topic can be found throughout the volumes of the encyclopedia

entry word: the word you look up in a dictionary

exclamation point: a punctuation mark used at the end of an interjection or an exclamatory sentence

exclamatory sentence: a type of sentence that shows strong surprise or emotion

expository report: a non-fiction genre that uses facts and details to inform or explain

F

fable: a genre of fiction that uses a story to get across a message or moral

fact: a statement that is true

fairy tale: a genre of fantasy fiction

false lead: an untrue clue in a mystery story that leads the reader or the main character away from the truth

fantasy: a type of fiction characterized by fantastic settings, characters, or action

fiction: a story or type of writing that is not true

figurative meaning/figurative language: something untrue that is said to make a point; a figure of speech

first person: main character tells the story from his or her point of view

foreshadowing: hints about what is going to happen later in the story

fragment: a group of words that does not tell or ask something; an incomplete sentence

free verse: poetry without a set rhyme scheme

friendly letter: an informal letter written to a friend or relative

future tense: verb tense that indicates action or a state of being that will take place

G

genre: a type of writing, such as fiction, mystery, or biography

gerund: a verb form ending in *ing* that functions as a noun

glossary: alphabetical listing of terms and vocabulary words found in a book, usually located at the back of a book

greeting: the way the writer says hello in a letter

guide words: words printed at the top of a dictionary page that are the first and last words found on that page

H

haiku: a 17 syllable poem of three lines with a nature theme

heading: address of the person who wrote the business letter

helping verb: a verb used with another verb to make a sentence clearer

historical fiction: a type of fiction that uses real settings and events from history to tell a fiction story

homographs: words that come from different roots that are spelled the same but have different meanings and even different pronunciations

homonyms: words that sound the same but have different meanings and spellings

hyperbole: exaggeration

hyphen: a punctuation mark used to hold words together

I

idiom: a figure of speech common to one language; a phrase that has a figurative meaning

imagery: writing with great use of description, so the reader can see what the author has written

imperative sentence: a type of sentence that gives a command

imported words: words used in English that came from other languages, such as French, Latin, or Japanese

indefinite adjective: an adjective that gives an approximate number or quantity or

that refers to no specific person or thing, but does not tell exactly how many or how much

indefinite pronoun: a pronoun that refers generally, not specifically, to people, places, or things

indent: several spaces used to mark the beginning of a paragraph

independent clause: a group of words with a subject and a predicate that expresses a complete thought and can stand by itself as a sentence

index: an alphabetical listing of topics and their page numbers found in the back of a book

indirect object: a word that tells "to whom" or "for whom" something is done

indirect quotation: a character or narrator tells the reader what another character said, without quotation marks

infinitive: a present tense verb preceded by the word *to* (to + verb = infinitive) that can act as a noun, an adjective, or an adverb

inside address: the name and address of the company to whom a business letter is written

intensifier: an adverb that modifies another adverb, telling how much

intensive pronoun: a pronoun that emphasizes, or intensifies, the noun or pronoun it refers to

interjection: a capitalized word followed by an exclamation point at the beginning of a sentence that shows emotion

interrogative pronoun: a pronoun that introduces a question

interrogative sentence: a type of sentence that asks a question

intransitive verb: a verb that does not need an object to complete its meaning frequently followed by a prepositional phrase

introductory phrase: a prepositional phrase that starts a sentence

irregular verb: a verb that forms its tense by a change in spelling or word form

italics: a slanted type used to identify books, movies, songs, titles, and many other proper nouns

K

key: explanation of the symbols on a map or chart

K-W-L chart: a brainstorming chart to organize what you know, want to know, and what you have learned about your topic

L

legend: explanation of the symbols on a map or chart

library catalog: a database of all the materials the library has that can be searched by author, title, subject, keyword, or call number

limerick: a five line poem with a specific rhyme scheme

linking verb: a verb that connects, or links, the subject of the sentence to a word or words in the predicate

literal meaning/literal language: the exact meaning of words

M

metaphor: a figure of speech that compares two things

mild interjection: an interjection used to show mild emotion that is not capitalized or followed by an exclamation point

misplaced modifier: a modifier that is not placed near the word or phrase that it modifies

modifier: word or a phrase that adds to the meaning of the sentence

monologue: a speech made by one character in a play, spoken to the audience alone, or to another character

multiple meaning words: words with more than one meaning

mystery: type of fiction where a crime must be solved

N

narrator: person who tells a story

non-fiction: a type of writing that is completely true

noun: a word that names a person, place, thing, or idea

noun clause: a dependent clause that functions as a noun used as a subject, a direct object, an indirect object, an object of a preposition, or a predicate noun

O

object of a preposition: a noun or pronoun that follows the preposition or prepositional phrase and relates the noun or pronoun to another word in the sentence

object pronoun: a pronoun that directly receives the action of the verb, indirectly receives the action of a verb, or is the object of a preposition.

onomatopoeia: a word that sounds like the sound it names, such as *buzz, snap*

opinion: a statement that explains a belief; not a fact

order of importance: organizing an expository report using the most important points first

outline: a list of the information gathered for a paper with topics (I, II, III, IV), subtopics (A, B, C), and details (1, 2, 3)

P

parallel construction: writing sentences with verbs and subjects that agree in gender and number, and keeping one verb tense throughout a sentence

parenthesis: punctuation marks used to separate information from the rest of the sentence

participial phrase: a group of words that includes the participle and its objects, complements, or modifiers

participle: a verb form that can function as an adjective

passive voice: when the subject receives the action or is the result of the action of the verb

past participle: the combination of the present tense of the helping verb *to have* plus the past tense of the verb it helps

past tense: a verb tense that indicates that an action or state of being has been completed

paragraph: a group of sentences that all support a main idea

parts of speech: categories of words based on how words are used in a sentence

period: a punctuation mark used to mark the end of a declarative or imperative sentence

periodicals: magazines, newspapers, and other writing that is published periodically, or every so often on a specific schedule

personal pronoun: a pronoun that names the speaker, the person spoken to, or the person or thing spoken about

personification: giving an inanimate object or an animal human qualities

persuasive essay: genre of non-fiction that uses facts and details to support the writer's argument; meant to encourage the reader to accept the writer's opinion or belief about the topic

plagiarism: passing off someone else's ideas as your own without giving that person credit; copying

play: a genre of fiction that uses characters to act out the plot

plot: the plan of action in a story; the problem that must be solved in a story

plural: more than one

poem: a type of writing that uses incomplete sentences and rhyme schemes to express feelings or create descriptions

point of view: the narrator's version of the events in a story

positive adjective: an adjective that describes a noun or pronoun without comparing it to anyone or anything else

positive adverb: an adverb that describes a noun, pronoun, or adjective without comparing it to anyone or anything else

possessive noun: a noun that shows ownership

possessive pronoun: a pronoun that shows ownership

predicate adjective: an adjective used a subject complement

predicate noun: a noun used as a subject complement

predicate pronoun: a pronoun used as a subject complement

predicate verb: the simple predicate of a sentence

prefix: one or more syllables added to the beginning of a word to change the word's meaning

preposition: a word that shows the position or relationship between a noun and another word

prepositional phrase: a group of words starting with a preposition that usually ends with a noun or pronoun and functions as an adjective or an adverb, depending on the word it modifies

present perfect tense: a verb tense formed using the present tense of the helping verb *to have* plus the past participle

present tense: a verb tense indicating action or a state of being that is happening now

prewriting: the first part of the writing process; deciding on a topic for a paper

problem-cause-solution: organizing an expository report by explaining the problem, the cause, and the solution according to the topic

pronoun: a word that takes the place of a noun

proofreader's marks: marks used to correct specific mistakes in grammar, punctuation, or capitalization

proofreading: the fourth part of the writing process; correcting mistakes in punctuation, capitalization, and grammar

proper noun: a noun that names a specific person, place, or thing

publishing: the fifth part of the writing process; making your finished work available for public viewing

Q

qualifier: an adverb that modifies another adverb, telling to what extent

question mark: a punctuation mark used at the end of an interrogative sentence

quotation: rewriting word for word what someone said or wrote, punctuated with quotation marks

quotation marks: punctuation marks used to indicate dialogue or a quotation, or a song title

R

rambling: not staying on topic; changing the subject often within a paragraph

realistic fiction: a fiction story that could happen in real life

reflexive pronoun: a pronoun that refers the action back to the noun or pronoun

reference: section of the library with dictionaries, thesauruses, encyclopedias, atlases, and other books that cannot be checked out but are there for all library goers to use

relative pronoun: the pronouns *that, which,* and *who*

research: using reference materials to find facts and details to include in your writing

revising: the third part of the writing process; editing the content of the paper

rhyme scheme: specific rhyming pattern used in a poem

root word: a word part from Greek or Latin

rubric: a list of things writing must do in order to get a certain grade

run-on: a sentence or paragraph that goes on and on without proper punctuation

S

scene: part of the action in a play

science fiction: a type of fiction that uses scientific findings and futuristic technology to build its setting and plot

second person: the reader is spoken to; the narrator tells the reader what the character does

semi-colon: a punctuation mark used to combine two independent clauses when a conjunction is not used

sensory words: words that describe the reaction of the five senses: smell, sight, touch, taste, and hearing

set: where a scene of a play takes place

setting: the location and time in which a story takes place

shades of meaning: subtle differences between the meanings of synonyms

signature: a person's signed name on a letter

simile: a figure of speech that compares two things using *like* or *as*

simple predicate: also called the predicate verb; the main verb or verb phrase in the complete predicate

simple sentence: a type of sentence that contains one independent clause

simple subject: the main word in the complete subject

singular: only one

skimming: fast reading to get the main idea and important points from a source

slang: informal words used to represent a formal noun or adjective

slash: a punctuation mark used to separate lines of poetry in a quotation

spine: part of the book that holds the pages together; where the title, author, publisher's information, and call number are written

split infinitive: an infinitive (to + present tense verb) written with *to* and separated from the verb

stage direction: instructions explaining what a character in a play should be doing while saying his or her lines

stet: a proofreader's correction that means leave as is

subject complement: a word that comes after a linking verb and refers back to the subject

subject pronoun: the pronoun to use when the pronoun is the subject of a sentence or clause or the pronoun follows a form of the verb *be* and renames the subject

subordinating conjunction: a conjunction that shows the connection between a dependent, or subordinating clause, and the rest of the sentence

suffix: a syllable, group of syllables, or word added to the end of a word to change its meaning or grammatical function

superlative adjective: an adjective that compares three or more things, people, places, or actions

superlative adverb: an adverb that compares three or more things, people, places, or actions

suspense: building of tension in a story

symbol: a literal thing, place, or happening in writing that has a figurative meaning

symbols: pictures or markings on a map that stand for different objects, cities, or landforms

synonyms: words that mean the same thing

T

table of contents: page at the beginning of a book listing chapter titles and the pages on which they start

tall tale: a genre of fiction that uses exaggeration to develop its characters or what they can do

theme: the main point or idea; the moral of a story

thesaurus: a reference book containing an alphabetical listing of words and their synonyms and antonyms

third person: the narrator tells what happens to the characters

title page: page at the beginning of a book that lists the author, title, and publisher's information

tone: the mood of the story

topic sentence: first sentence of a paragraph; gives the main idea of the paragraph

transitive verb: an action verb that is followed by a direct object

transition words: words that show time or compare and contrast; transition words help to introduce a new idea

transpose: a proofreader's correction that means to switch a word or sentence or paragraph with another word, sentence, or paragraph

U

underline: a line written under the hand-written title of a book

V

verb: a word that shows action or a state of being

verb phrase: a phrase that contains one or more helping verbs along with the main verb

W

writing process: the five-step plan for prewriting, drafting, revising, proofreading, and publishing a paper

Things to Write About

Story Web

Complete the web below. Write a word in each oval that tells something about the words in the middle. Use the web to write a story on the next page.

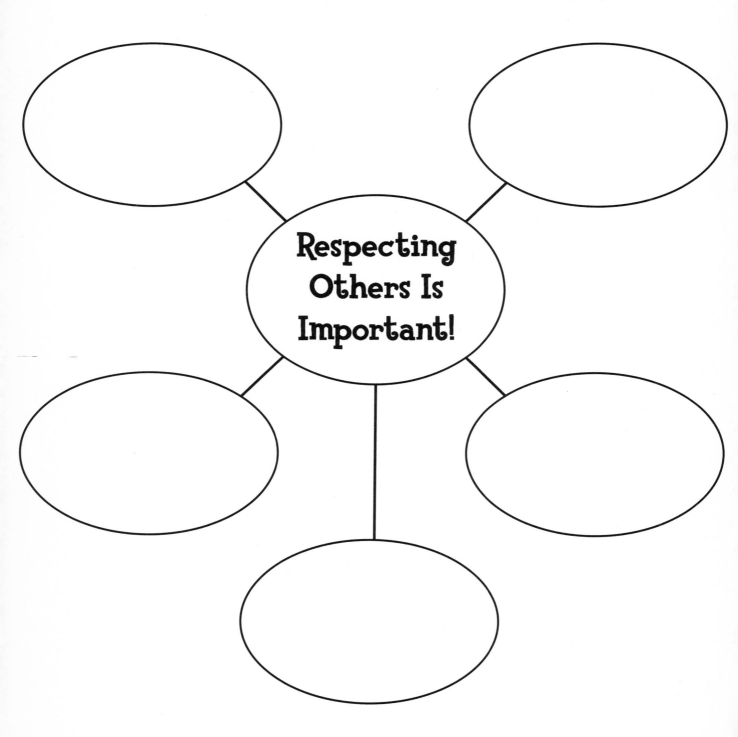

Respecting Others Is Important!

Respecting Others Is Important!

Use the web on the previous page. Write a story about why respecting others is important. Use complete sentences.

_____

_____

_____

_____

_____

_____

_____

_____

_____

_____

_____

_____

R-E-S-P-E-C-T

Make a list of ten ways that you can show respect to your classmates.

1. _____

2. _____

3. _____

4. _____

5. _____

6. _____

7. _____

8. _____

9. _____

10. _____

What Does It Mean?

What song means the most to you? Name your special song. Then, explain why this song is important to you.

_____

Song Title

_____

_____

_____

_____

_____

_____

_____

_____

_____

_____

_____

Healthy Snacks

Make a list of ten healthy snacks that you can make yourself.

1. _____

2. _____

3. _____

4. _____

5. _____

6. _____

7. _____

8. _____

9. _____

10. _____

Something New

Think about a time when you tried something that you had never done before. Write a story about what you did and how you felt. Use complete sentences.

_____

_____

_____

_____

_____

_____

_____

_____

_____

_____

_____

_____

_____

_____

A Silly Song

Think about a situation that made you laugh out loud. Tell your silly story in a song. Write your lyrics to a familiar tune, such as "Row, Row, Row Your Boat." Give your song a title.

_____

Song Title

_____

_____

_____

_____

_____

_____

_____

_____

_____

_____

_____

Campfire Songs

Pretend that you are camping with your family. You are sitting around a campfire singing songs. Write a story about your experience. Use complete sentences.

_____

_____

_____

_____

_____

_____

_____

_____

_____

_____

_____

_____

_____

A Warm Welcome

Imagine that you are visiting a foreign country for the first time. You do not speak the language. Write a story about how the citizens of this country make you feel welcome. Use complete sentences.

_____

_____

_____

_____

_____

_____

_____

_____

_____

_____

_____

_____

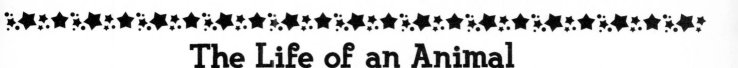

The Life of an Animal

If you were an animal, which one would you be? Name an animal, and write a story about your life as that animal. Use complete sentences.

_____
Animal

_____

_____

_____

_____

_____

_____

_____

_____

_____

_____

_____

_____

Music and Friends

Do you and your friends ever sing songs together? Write a story about a time when you and your friends sang together. Use complete sentences.

_____

_____

_____

_____

_____

_____

_____

_____

_____

_____

_____

_____

_____

_____

His Name-O!

Make up a song about one of your friends to the tune of "B-I-N-G-O." To help you, the first stanza of the song is in the box below.

B-I-N-G-O

There was a farmer who had a dog,
And Bingo was his name-o.
B-I-N-G-O
B-I-N-G-O
B-I-N-G-O
And Bingo was his name-o!

_____

_____

_____

_____

_____

_____

_____

_____

Classroom Chaos?

Write a story about what your classroom would be like if no one cooperated, including your teacher. Use complete sentences.

_____

_____

_____

_____

_____

_____

_____

_____

_____

_____

_____

_____

_____

You Can Depend on Me

Describe a time when someone depended on you, and you proved you were responsible. What did you do? How did you feel? Use complete sentences.

_____

_____

_____

_____

_____

_____

_____

_____

_____

_____

_____

_____

_____

You Can Count on Me

List ten ways that you show people you are responsible.

1._____

2._____

3._____

4._____

5._____

6._____

7._____

8._____

9._____

10._____